# The Hunt for the Buru

# The Hunt for the Buru

The true story of the search
for a prehistoric reptile in North India

by
Ralph Izzard

A Craven Street Book
Linden Publishing
Fresno, CA

# THE HUNT FOR THE BURU

by

Ralph Izzard

Cover art by James Goold

124689753
ISBN 0-941936-65-1

Originally published by Hoddard & Stoughton Ltd., London England 1951

Library of Congress Cataloging-in-Publication Data

Izzard, Ralph.
　　The Hunt for the Buru / By Ralph Izzard.
　　　　p.cm.
　　"A Craven Street Book"
　　Originally published: London : Hodder & Stoughton, 1951.
　　ISBN 0-941936-65-1
　　1. Assam (India)--Description and travel. 2. Animals, Mythical. I. Title.

DS485.A84 I84 2001
915.4'162042--dc21

2001016448

**A Craven Street Book**

Linden Publishing Inc.
2000 South Mary, Fresno CA 93721 USA
800-345-4447   www.lindenpub.com

# Ralph Izzard
# A Friend and Chronicler of Crypotozoology

Ralph William Burdick Izzard was an adventurer, a romantic, a writer, and a journalist. Within the annals of cryptozoology, the study of hidden animals yet to be discovered by science, Izzard was an important member and chronicler of some significant expeditions. One was the search for the Buru, which you will learn about as you read this excellent book, and the other was in his quest for the Yeti, the Abominable Snowmen of the Himalaya. Intriguingly, Ralph Izzard was also the friend to some pivotal characters in the early days of cryptozoology.

Izzard's straightforward biography reads like many journalistically minded young men of his day. He was educated at Cambridge where he graduated in 1931. That same year, he joined the staff of the Daily Mail of London and his first assignments as foreign correspondent sent him to Berlin and Prague. During World War II he joined the RNVR as an Ordinary Seaman, qualified as a gunner, and was offered a commission. He gained honorable mention in dispatches and was awarded the OBE. On demobilization, he went back to the Daily Mail as foreign correspondent in New Delhi, Washington D.C., and Cairo and as the war correspondent in Korea. But Izzard's cryptozoological connections came from his schoolboy days, and followed him through his life, on a parallel path to his newspaper work.

Attending Cambridge University in England in 1928-1931, Ralph Izzard met and became lifelong friends of schoolmates Ivan T. Sanderson and Gerald Russell. Who were Sanderson and Russell?

Ivan Terence Sanderson, one of the foremost pioneers of cryptozoology, was born in Edinburgh, Scotland. Sanderson led expeditions to some of the world's remotest jungles, gathering interesting tales on a wide variety of animals. Sanderson's early books were keen portrayals of natural history information that became extremely popular and included

*Animal Treasure* (1937), *Caribbean Treasure* (1939), *Living Treasure* (1941), *Animal Tales* (1946), *Living Mammals of the World* (1955), *Follow the Whale* (1956), and *Monkey Kingdom* (1957). In the 1940's, Sanderson began to write in the *Saturday Evening Post* on topics ranging from sea monsters to living dinosaurs. One of these articles inspired "The Father of Crypotozoology" Bernard Heuvelmans's interest in pursuing cryptozoology. Heuvelmans's classic book, *On the Track of Unknown Animals* (1955) would become the early bible of cryptozoology. Sanderson's *Abominable Snowmen: Legend Come to Life* (1961), the seminal work on the subject, remains a useful reference book. The 525-page book brought notice to the global nature of the reports of Yeti, Bigfoot, and other giant hairy hominoid creatures. Sanderson remained a close friend and associate of Ralph Izzard, consulting with him on all types of cryptids including the Buru and the Yeti, up to Sanderson's death in 1973.

Gerald Russell is best known for his role with Izzard and adventurer Tom Slick in important Himalayan Yeti expeditions in the 1950's. Russell was an explorer who seemed always available for whatever cryptozoological pursuit came his way from the 1930's through the late 1950's. In 1932 Russell went with Sanderson as a member of the Percy Sladen expedition to Africa. While there, in the British Cameroons, in high forests, at the Mainyu river near the Mamfe Pool, they encountered a large unknown animal, called *mbulu-em'bembe* (or Mokele-mbembe in the cryptozoological literature of today). Two months later, in the Assumbo Mountains, they witnessed the overflight of a giant batlike animal, known locally as an *oliliau* (more commonly known as the Kongamato).

During 1933-34 Russell participated in the William Harvest Harkness Asiatic Expedition to Tibet in pursuit of the giant panda. While this particular expedition was unsuccessful, he returned in 1936-37, with the W.H., then Ruth Harkness Asiatic Expedition to Tibet, and assisted in capturing the first giant panda. Richard Parry in his *The World of the Giant Panda* writes, "W. M. Russell obtained a half-grown tame beisung (giant panda), which was wandering free on a

Wassu farm and apparently thriving on grass and other vegetation."

In 1939, while living in New York, Russell was one of the first Americans to volunteer for service with the British Royal Navy, and saw action in the Mediterranean and the Normandy landings. Russell ran into Izzard in occupied Hamburg in 1945. It was always a small world for Izzard, Russell and Sanderson.

During the three years after World War II Russell journeyed to China to attempt to capture a rare, little known animal, the golden takin, but was forced to abandon his efforts because of the advance of the Chinese Communist army. The early years of the 1950's found Russell making a series of films on native methods of catching wild animals in Asia and Europe. When the planning of the 1954 *Daily Mail* expedition to Nepal in search of the Yeti began, Ralph Izzard naturally recommended that Russell be picked as one of the leaders. Over 300 men were part of the expedition, including Russell, Dr. Charles Stoner, Dr. Bisaway Biswas, Tom Stobart, John A. Jackson, and yes, of course, Izzard. Russell was able to collect good sightings and droppings of the smallest type of Yeti, Teh-lma, seen in the montane forests of Nepal. This third type of Yeti, the Teh-lma, seems related to other anthropoids, the Proto-Pygmies, reported from throughout some of the mountainous tropical valleys of Oriental Asia. Gerald Russell's and Ralph Izzard's experiences with the *Daily Mail* expedition of 1954, produced much evidence for the reality of the Teh-lma's presence (footprints, sightings, and feces). In 1955, Izzard would write *The Abominable Snowman Adventure* to record what took place on the expedition. Some forty years ago, the Teh-lma was the major Yeti that was seen and discussed by zoologists who thought it would be soon caught. Sadly, by 1960, most of the funding for Yeti expeditions had dried up. The Teh-lma remains elusive still.

Tom Slick, who would sponsor serious but quiet efforts to find the Yeti, heard of Russell's abilities through Izzard's writings. As I was writing *Tom Slick and the Search for the Yeti* (Boston: Faber and Faber, 1989), I exchanged correspondence with Ralph Izzard, who told me that he would often meet with Slick to discuss Yeti. Izzard's wry humor came through in the letters, and he noted, with a wink, that he thought Slick was more interested in capturing a female Yeti than a male one. Izzard, of course, was an obvious choice for Slick to gather information on Yeti, because of Izzard's 1954 expedition experiences. In 1958 Russell would lead the Slick-Johnson Snowman Expedition to Nepal, based in large part on Izzard's and Sanderson's recommendations. Russell and his Sherpa companion Da Temba saw one of the little Teh-lma in the upper Arun Valley of Nepal during the Slick trek.

Izzard's love of the Orient's cryptids, nevertheless, began long before his Yeti adventures. First there was the Buru.

The Buru is a large, unknown monitor lizard reported in remote valleys of the Himalaya of Assam, a province in the northeastern corner of India. Reported routinely during the 1940's, Burus allegedly looked, in most descriptions, something like a 20-foot aquatic version of the Komodo Dragon. Witnesses who heard them said they emitted hoarse, bellowing calls.

In 1948, Ralph Izzard's *Daily Mail* dispatched the Buru Expedition with the hope that it would return with physical evidence of the animals. The expedition's members included such notables as Charles Stonor, a professional zoologist, and of course, Ralph Izzard, who would later write *The Hunt for the Buru* (1951)– reprinted in this version for the first time since then. The expedition heard enough testimony of earlier encounters to persuade Bernard Heuvelmans that these unidentified monitors may be only recently extinct. Heuvelmans pointed out during the 1980's, that current sightings describe a similar regional beast, what the natives call a jhoor, from the Gir region of India. Other sightings of large, unknown monitor lizards are known in Bhutan, whose king claims to have seen one, and in Burma.

The Buru may be still out there, after all, in one geographical subspecies or another, near the same valleys that Izzard searched a half century ago. For now, read this wonderful chronicle of his quest, and wonder.

*Loren Coleman, January 2001*
*Professor, University of Southern Maine*

# ACKNOWLEDGEMENTS

This is the story of a fantastic adventure made possible by the generosity of a number of persons.

Firstly, I am very greatly indebted to Associated Newspapers Ltd., owners of the Daily Mail, for enabling me to take part in the Buru expedition and write this book. Also for permission to reproduce photographs.

J. P. Mills, M.A., C.S.I., C.I.E., one of the greatest living authorities on the tribes of the Assam Frontier, has made an important contribution by making available to me his share of the manuscript which forms my Chapter II. He very kindly agreed that this manuscript should not be published elsewhere until it has first appeared in this book.

Finally, this book would never have been written had it not been for the enthusiasm and encouragement of C. R. S. Stonor, B.Sc., who was the mainspring of the whole expedition. If anthropologists find anything of value in the book concerning the life and habits of little-known tribes, the credit is entirely due to Mr. Stonor. The errors are all mine.

RALPH IZZARD

FOR

PERCY AND MILES IZZARD

# CONTENTS

# CHAPTER I

# How it Began

A FEW YEARS AGO I SHOULD HAVE HAD TO BEGIN THIS story by explaining that Assam is a province in the remote north-east corner of India. That can no longer be necessary, for during the war Assam became known to the world as the 'build up' area for the Burma Front. An endless succession of British and American troops passed across the province on their way to and from Calcutta. In the East they operated in country, and among tribes, previously only known to a handful of political officers and anthropologists. Much of the mystery of that part of the province was dissipated by the exigencies of war. But when peace came an area of northern Assam, many thousands of square miles in extent, remained untouched, scarcely penetrated.

It was from the blue hills of this region that, in the spring of 1948, news came of what promised to be a first-class sensation. An "extinct" monster had been seen striding along the Himalayan border! Reports had been sent to the Royal Zoological Society in London—the services of experts had been engaged to track down the "monster" and report upon it. How much of this was true? The original newspaper report gave the "monster" such preposterous size and shape that zoologists rightly discounted it at once. But I am here to state that there was every reason to believe that a hitherto unknown creature, of more modest dimensions, *did* exist, for I was one of a party of three who set out with official sponsorship and the encouragement of eminent scientists, to trace it. With me went Charles Stonor, a professional zoologist, and Frank Hodgkinson, expert cameraman. It was unfortunate for us that the

9

news broke upon the world while the three of us were still engaged in the chase and completely out of touch with civilisation.

We had no control over the initial report, we would have suppressed it had we been able: but now, for the first time I can tell the full story.

For me it all began in the conventional manner of fiction, which was why, in my own mind, I dared to think it might have a conventional happy ending.

The scene was a bungalow in Delhi in winter; an excellent dinner, brandy and cigars in front of a bright log fire. Opposite me, across the hearth, sat A. P. F. Hamilton of the Indian Forestry Service, the firelight gleaming on his immaculate shirt front. Hamilton had graduated to a Delhi bungalow after very many years spent in the wilderness. Now, in his fifties, greying, but of tough and wiry build, he was still full of boyish enthusiasm for travel in strange places.

I had just remarked that it was a thousand pities that so little of the earth was left to explore.

"I wouldn't be so sure," said Hamilton, reaching for a cigar and lighting it.

"Now down in Shillong there's a fellow named Stonor who claims to have discovered a 'Lost Valley' up in Northern Assam—says it's a burial ground of prehistoric animals—Conan Doyle sort of stuff—thinks there may be a Saurian there, too, which buries itself in the mud during the winter and emerges when the summer monsoon comes—if I had my time over again I'd be up there like a shot—good fellow Stonor—sound, reliable sort of chap."

It took some time for this information to sink in, but as soon as I realised the possibilities of it I pestered Hamilton with questions. Little did either of us then realise what his chance remarks would lead to, but once on the scent I was not to be put off.

That night I decided to take a chance and that is how, next day, I came to be addressing a letter to:

C. R. Stonor,
Agricultural Officer,
North-East Frontier
Tribal Area, Shillong, Assam.

DEAR STONOR (I wrote),

You may well think this a strange letter; my excuse for writing it is a recent after-dinner conversation with Hamilton of the Indian Forestry Service, who I believe is known to you. I am the representative in India of the London *Daily Mail*. We had been discussing expeditions to remote places, when Hamilton brought up the subject of a "lost valley" in Assam, which he says you have visited, and which may be a graveyard of prehistoric animals, and the home of an unidentified Saurian which hibernates during the dry season and emerges when the rains come.

In the sober light of day, as Hamilton agrees, the story sounds rather fantastic—like something out of Conan Doyle or H. G. Wells—but if there is a chance of even a minor scientific success I would be prepared to have a shot at it. Would it be troubling you too much to let me have: (*a*) your opinion as to whether there is any sense at all in organising a small expedition? (*b*) a brief outline as to what such an expedition would entail? Details can be worked out later, and I am prepared to come to Shillong to seek your advice should you consider the idea worth pursuing.

My own idea would be to organise a small reconnaissance party consisting of say:

1. An officer with knowledge of local terrain and conditions.
2. A British Officer formerly with the Indian Army to organise labour, etc. (I could probably find someone who has been through the Burma Campaign, but it might be possible to combine 1 and 2.)
3. A Zoologist.
4. Myself.

I have no doubt that if this party came back with something

positive to report plenty of money would be available to support a more ambitious expedition.  At the first attempt I should like to travel as light as possible, and to waste the minimum amount of time in getting to the actual site.

Above all, I should value your opinion as to whether you think we are merely dealing with a local legend or are chasing something with a reasonable basis of fact behind it.

Please forgive me if, as I fear, I am merely wasting your time.

Yours sincerely,<br>
RALPH IZZARD.

As soon as I had walked across the road and posted that letter I was beset with doubts and fears.  Hamilton, although a sound enough man himself, might have got hold of the wrong end of the stick.  Stonor, in a subsequent expedition might already have exploded his own theory.  In any case it would be hard to convince the *Daily Mail* office in London, that the story to be got from some prehistoric remains was worth the labour and expense of digging them up.  Their attitude was likely to be: "Let Stonor produce the goods; then we'll buy the story."

Nevertheless, I felt a certain guilty satisfaction in having, at least, made an attempt to shake off the shackles and conventions of society and escape from the formal garden city atmosphere of New Delhi.

The cinema, the novel and strip-cartoon tend to over-glamourise the life of a Foreign Correspondent.  If the truth be known, his "big stories" are all too often a few isolated italicised sentences in a bulky humdrum chapter, largely made up of interpretations of political hand-outs, reports of interviews and conferences, re-hashes of extracts from local newspapers.  More often than not he is as closely tied to the capital of a country as a merchant seaman is tied to its ports.  That had certainly been my lot in India.  I had arrived nearly two years before with the Cabinet Mission, instructed to cover the political crisis involved in the surrender of power to Indian hands. I watched that crisis develop along its painful course until in August, 1947, India had emerged triumphantly, if shakily, as an independent Dominion. What had happened subsequently was anticlimax; the main task was completed. And all the time I had scarcely been away from Delhi for more than a week or two at a stretch! I had seen little enough of provincial India; I had done nothing towards fulfilling a boyhood ambition to be out and away off the beaten track, probing into the few remaining areas of the world where no white man had ever been before.

Now, if I had the wit to seize it, the ability to organise enough of both time and money, had come a heaven-sent chance!

My main fear was that Stonor might fail me; the fact that I had already committed myself by writing to him so confidently worried me less. The romance of the mysterious "lost valley" had gripped me so completely that I was already working out an alternative plan should my London office decide not to back me. My spell of duty in Delhi was to end in any case by the end of March. I was then due to be relieved. It was planned that I should spend two or three months' leave in England before taking up another post on the other side of the world. Why should I not spend my leave in Assam? That would take care of the time factor; all that would then be necessary would be to scrape enough money of my own together to finance the expedition; then I should be free to approach London on a "pay by results" basis.

Anxiously I waited for Stonor's reply. With its coming all my fears vanished for his letter contained better, far better, news than I had dared to hope for.

DEAR IZZARD (he wrote),

I was more than interested to receive your letter concerning our monster, about which you heard from Hamilton.

The position is that there are two areas involved: (i) where there is a very credible tradition of a beast, which even goes to the length of pointing out burial sites. I have twice been there with J. P. Mills, and our joint account of the tradition is awaiting publication in a scientific journal. The excavation of the sites is a big matter, and would call for a special expedition. I will try and send you a copy of the manuscript.

(ii) The second area is fifty miles distant over several ranges, and I am the only European who has actually been there. It is here the beast is said to live. I was there in the cold weather, when they were hibernating beneath a quite inaccessible swamp; so my tale is based on the verbal reports of about thirty tribes-people who have seen them.

Personally I am quite convinced that the whole thing is 100 per cent true. . . . The only answer is to go up and see the beasts and try for photographs. There are two main snags.

(i) Porters. I am now trying to find a way round that.

(ii) Entry and exit to the plains is more or less blocked during the rains, and it might mean going up not later than mid-April and staying put until about August.

I *hope* to be free to go up in six or seven weeks time (end March, 1948) if snags can be got over, and it would be very nice if you could come too. I therefore wired you to-day. My own position is that I want to get there so as to get enough proof to get a full-scale expedition sent. I am not interested in "cashing in" on it, but as the pioneer, I naturally would like the credit for the *scientific* aspect of the find. If your employers would finance the initial trip, it would be very nice, and exclusive rights of publicity, etc. would not worry me at all. For the initial trip to get proof I am not in favour of more than two members of the party, preferably "our good selves".

What the beast is, assuming it to be there, I cannot say. It must be a reptile, and is said to be the size of an ox, with a prominent snout. One suggestion is that it is some sort of primitive crocodilian; it *might* even be a dinosaur. I don't want to drag you on a wild goose, or Loch Ness monster chase: but I can't see how the matter can be other than true. If you can come here between the 4th and 15th March, I can arrange accommodation in this hotel, and there is a daily air-service from Calcutta to Gauhati, which is three hours run from here. I can let you have the whole tale then.

                              Yours sincerely,
                              C. R. STONOR.

*Please keep it confidential at present!*

As I read that letter I felt a warm glow rise within me as if I had drained a glass of wine. The "lost valley" was not then, merely a "valley of dried bones"! It was the haunt of a real live flesh and blood reptile of unknown species and of considerable size! Previously I had thought of the Saurian mentioned by Hamilton in terms of a lizard say, a couple of feet long. But Stonor himself had dubbed it a "monster", and given it the bulk of an ox. Surely the prospect of con-tributing to the discovery of a hitherto unknown major animal, possibly the outstanding zoological discovery of the century, would be irresistible to London! It did not *have* to be a dinosaur; but how much better if it were! Then there was an additional cause for congratulation. It had seemed too much to expect that Stonor, himself, would be available for another expedition so I had not ventured the hope in my first letter to him. But not only was he willing to make the attempt; it appeared that he was actually planning it, and what was more, he was due to start almost to the day when I should be free of the ties of Delhi, free to join him!

Nevertheless, with so much in my favour I still felt incap-able of presenting an adequate case by cable, so I sat down and wrote a soberly worded letter to London setting out exactly what I thought would be involved.

In the first place, and most important, we had Stonor with us. It would not mean sending off an expensive expedition to spend months if not years searching a thous-and square miles of difficult mountain country in the hope of finally running the animal down. Stonor was the one man in the world who could pin-point the exact swamp where the monster was alleged to dwell. He could lead the pair of us straight there; in addition, he was acquainted with the local terrain and conditions; could no doubt cope with the local tribal dialects. He was a "one-man expedition" in himself; and that fact would slash the over-all costs enormously. (I was to learn later that Stonor had many other qualities. Before taking up his present appointment he had been a professional zoologist: for some years he had specialised in tribal ethnology.)

With the party reduced to two there was no fear of a leakage of information. Also, as the animal apparently only showed itself for a short summer season, we should return with a complete monopoly of knowledge concerning it, and would have nearly a full year in which to exploit our advantage. This was emphasising the commercial aspect of the monster, but this I felt bound to do if we were to expect any support. But whichever way you looked at the monster the expedition seemed to me worth while. Even should the monster fail to materialise, the mere fact that we had launched after it an expedition into unexplored country among little known tribes was a "story" in itself.

While this letter was wending its dilatory way to London by air mail, Stonor and I continued corresponding both by letter and cable. I took a further chance in telling him that I felt reasonably sure support would be forthcoming. Back came another letter, with two bulky enclosures.

The covering letter ran:

DEAR IZZARD,

I was very glad to get your wire and hear that you hope to come to Shillong on 9–10th March. It is only fair that you should see all the information available and form your own judgment. I therefore enclose copies of notes. The account of the tradition of the Apa Thanis has been sent in by Mills and myself to the Anthropological Institute for publication as a tradition on its own merits.

The other account is still a dark and deadly secret.

Other people's opinions to whom these accounts have been sent are:

1. W. D. Lang, Sc.D., F.R.S. (an international palaeontologist). Appears completely convinced and suggests that the beast may be some sort of primitive crocodilian.

2. Professor D. M. S. Watson, D.Sc., F.R.S., "We have heard of this sort of thing before."

3. N. B. Kinnear (Director of the Natural History Museum, London). "Most people seem to think that there is some unknown animal; but not necessarily a prehistoric monster."

4. Sir D'Arcy Thompson, C.B., D.C.L., LL.D., F.R.S. etc.: "You would be foolish indeed if you did not visit the place again. . . . all you want is one cast of one footprint or six inches of scaly skin."

Personally, I am convinced against my will that we are on the track of something quite fantastic.

To get down to hard facts. I am determined to get up there this season, by hook or crook. I am unlikely to be in India next year, and by the way things are going, unless it is done *now*, I don't think it ever will be. For climatic reasons it will be necessary to start *very early in April* and as I may have told you, it may mean being stuck up there till about August. On the other hand, there would be a reasonable chance of getting down before—at the cost of jettisoning equipment. I sincerely hope you can make it, and I do urge you to use all possible means to make the trip possible.

As far as finance goes: I reckon the total expenses for a short trip of just ourselves would be covered by £300. That would include porters, rations, a collapsible boat, hire of transport to the Base, presents for head-men, etc. In addition, a very important item is photographic apparatus, and most particularly a *powerful telescopic lens*. I would naturally want help over this. Possibly a camera could be loaned. My own is a simple one. I have a good telescope of my own.

Even if porters are not forthcoming I am going to try and go alone; but unless one has the necessary photographic apparatus, a folding boat, etc. it will be hard indeed to get enough evidence to convince the outside world.

I should add it is not a picnic party up there. The rainfall from late May to August is pretty fierce. There is, however, no question of getting mixed up in tribal wars.

Paludrine, and M & B will be efficient safeguards against sickness.

Yours sincerely,
C. R. STONOR.

*Do remember time is short and it is now or never!*

P.S. The burial sites in the Apa Tani area are best left until the living beast is proved.

The first enclosure was a bulky document, but I sat down and read it on the spot. I here reproduce it in full, for to appreciate our emotions throughout the chase it is necessary to know what evidence we were working on and why, through a number of depressing set-backs, we remained confident of final success.

# CHAPTER II

# The Burus of the Apa Tani Valley

A TRADITIONAL ACCOUNT OF THE SURVIVAL WITHIN
HISTORIC TIMES OF A LARGE AQUATIC REPTILE IN THE
OUTER HIMALAYAS OF ASSAM

By *J. P. MILLS, M.A., C.S.I., C.I.E., and C. R. S. STONOR, B.Sc.*

PART I

(1) INTRODUCTORY

When in the country of the Apa Tani tribe during the latter part of 1945, and again in 1946, we received from men whose ancestors were said to have seen them, a remarkable account of a species of extinct Saurian. We were further shown the exact sites where, according to most precise tradition, four were destroyed and buried.

(2) GEOGRAPHY OF THE AREA

The Apa Tani tribe is confined to an upland valley, approximately sixteen hundred metres above sea-level, situated in the outer Himalayas of the North-East Frontier of India, at approximately lat. 27° 35″ North, and long. 93° 50″ East. The whole area of the valley, which is surrounded by mountain ranges of two to three thousand metres in height, is 32 square kilometres or rather more: the central area with which we are concerned, consisting of approximately level, irrigated rice-fields. This cultivated area is some ten kilometres long, with a breadth, in places, of five kilometres. It is very irregular in shape, with innumerable large and small inlets of flat land running in between low projecting and bracken-covered spurs, on which the

19

seven large villages of the tribe are situated. The valley is, in effect, an elevated plateau surrounded by a rim of mountains, and lies between two river valleys: that of the Kamla to the north, and that of the Panior (or Panir) to the south, both of which are some six hundred metres below it. There is no area comparable with it in this region of the Himalayas, and it is reminiscent on a miniature scale of the great valley of Nepal.

The centre of the plateau is quite clearly a drained lake or swamp, the whole of which is now utilised for irrigated rice cultivation, with the exception of a small area at the south end which is a waterlogged, shallow swamp. The plateau is roughly bisected longitudinally by the Kal River, a small stream rising in the north-east section of the surrounding hills, and leaving the plateau at its southern end to join the Panior River some miles to the south. In the plateau itself the Kal River is a stream of moderate speed, running between low banks which are largely artificial, and winding through the cultivated paddy swamp.

It leaves the valley by an extremely narrow gap, and thereafter becomes a mountain torrent which rushes down a deep valley. The south end of the valley is closed except for the narrow outlet of the Kal River. Neither the Apa Tani Plateau or the surrounding country has ever been surveyed, but from superficial observation of artificial drains and ditches, and of the swamp itself, the bed of the valley appears to consist of a thick layer of silt superimposed on gravel. The climate is sub-temperate, with winter frosts and regular falls of snow.

## (3) THE APA TANI TRIBE

The Apa Tani tribe, with a population estimated at twenty thousand, is entirely confined to this one upland valley: the surrounding region being occupied by the Dafla tribe, a people still semi-nomadic and very probably later immigrants than the Apa Tanis.

Previous to 1944 only two expeditions had passed the verge of the Apa Tani Valley, at long intervals, and without making any effective contact with the people.

In 1944 and 1945, Dr. C. von Fürer-Haimendorf made the first detailed investigation of the tribe. His work is still unpublished, but he very kindly lent us the relevant notes, in which he records the tradition that the tribe migrated at an unknown date in its previous history from a former home in the Eastern Himalayas, and reached their present area after a journey through country then practically uninhabited; and were thus established before the infiltration of the Dafla tribes who now surround them.

On their arrival they found the valley a swampy lake in which, to quote Dr. von Fürer-Haimendorf's notes, "were snakes and monsters". We were led to make our own investigations by this recorded tradition. The languages of the Tibet-Burman group, to which Apa Tani presumably belongs, are poor in general terms, and it seemed more than probable that the expression "monsters" represented an attempt to translate something more precise.

We therefore followed up this clue, and at once discovered that the Apa Tani word BURU which had been translated by the vague terms "monsters" meant one particular beast of which a vivid tribal memory survived.

It is most important, if the tradition we are investigating is to be considered in its context (and to consider any tradition otherwise is a manifest absurdity), to bear in mind throughout the state of culture and general social level of the Apa Tani tribe. They are a primitive people of the same type of organisation as the Naga tribe of the Assam-Burma border, and the Abor and other tribes of the adjacent Himalayan region. They have no knowledge of writing, no art whatever, and their religion is a simple form of pure Animism without the slightest discernible admixture of Buddhism or Hinduism. Their political organisation is of the same corporate type as that of the Naga tribes, with some of whom they show considerable similarity in their material culture. They are, first and foremost, agriculturists, and have developed the natural fertility and resources of their valley to a remarkable degree, quite comparable with the advanced husbandry of the Angami Nagas. They are clearly people of high intelligence: their husbandry is ample testimony of this. By disposition they are dour, hard-headed, and unimaginative cultivators with their full share of the proverbial cupidity of the peasant. Their isolation is quite remarkable: a great many never leave the narrow confines of their own small valley, and the tribe seems to have founded no off-shoots in the surrounding region. Money is unknown to them, but parties do go down to the Plains of Assam during the cold season (a journey of several days over mountain paths) for trade and barter. These are mainly the poorer men, and most of the richer people seldom if ever leave their valley. There is a very little indirect trade with Tibet through other tribes, but no immediate contact. Otherwise the isolation of the Apa Tanis is, and has long been, virtually complete. No traders from the Plains are known to have visited the valley and there is no trace of modern Assamese culture. Although the plateau is comparatively near the Plains in a direct line, the intervening terrain of mountain ranges is very difficult, and until very recent years, the suspicious attitude of the Daflas has made penetration of their country without an armed escort impossible.

### (4) DESCRIPTION OF THE TRADITIONAL SAURIAN OR BURU

We first visited the valley in November 1945, when the following traditional description was given us by leading men of several villages, who were questioned separately and at intervals. We worked through the medium of reliable interpreters, who were employed with the greatest care. Neither our interpreters or the informants had any inkling of the possible scientific interest of their tradition, and there can be no question of their having embroidered their accounts to suit preconceived notions. For the sake of clarity we have given measure in centimetres and metres, but it must be clearly understood that the only standards of measurement known to the Apa Tanis are in terms of parts of the body, such as the forearm, the height of a man, the outstretched arm, etc.

The tradition, handed down verbally, is as follows:

When the Apa Tanis first came to the valley they found it filled with a great swampy lake, inhabited by large water animals, to which they gave the name of *Buru*. They had never seen a *buru*, either previously in their original home, or during their wanderings.

The length of a *buru* was about three and a half to four metres, and it was "long shaped". The *head* was about fifty centimetres long, and was elongated into a great snout, flattened at the tip. The eyes were behind the snout. The teeth were "flat like those of a man", except for a pair in the upper and lower jaws, which were large and pointed "like those of a tiger or a boar". The *neck* was rather under a metre in length, and could be stretched out or drawn in: (this was vividly explained by pantomime). The *body* was roundish "the breadth of a man's arm and body across the back", and with a girth "such as a man could just put his arms round". The *tail* was rounded and tapering, and about one and a half metres in length. The general opinion is that it was not very pointed. It was fringed "from where the animal excreted" (i.e. the base) with broad and deeply fringed lobes which ran the whole length on either side, and sprang from the dorsal surface of the tail. (The form and position of the lobes were demonstrated by placing leaves snipped to shape along the sides of a stick.) The *legs* were fifty centimetres long, with claws on the feet, and they and the feet looked like "the forefeet of a burrowing mole". The *skin* was like that of a scale-less fish. There were no hairs, but three lines of short, blunt spines ran down the back and along each side. The colour was dark blue blotched with white, and a broad band of white ran down the belly.

## (5) THE HABITS OF THE BURU

The *buru* lived entirely in the water, and never came to land. They were not often seen as they lived in water deeper than the height of a man. They used to put their necks up out of the water and make a hoarse bellowing noise: (this was imitated by our informants). Sometimes they were seen nosing in the muddy banks of the lake, and when doing so they waved their head and neck from side to side: (this was demonstrated by pantomime).

They did not kill or eat men, and it is believed they did not eat fish, but "lived on the mud". Nothing is known of their young or of their breeding habits.

## (6) THE BURU AT DUTA LAPANG

Once a man of the Tagomi clan, which still exists, and belonging to the village of Duta, which also still exists, went with his wife and family to live away from his village, and built a house on the extreme edge of the lake, at a spot now called *Duta Lapang*. During heavy rain, the bank gave way and the house with five people in it collapsed into the water, and they were all drowned. There was a *buru* nosing about in the mud at the time, and the house fell on top of it. The accident was seen by a boy who had left the house to answer the calls of nature. The *buru* was not seen again, and it is not known if it was killed.

## (7) THE KILLING OF THE BURUS

The ancestors of the Apa Tanis began to drain the lake by opening up the outlet whereby the Kal stream leaves the valley. As the ground was drained it was turned into rice fields, and as time went on, there was less and less water deep enough for the *burus* to live in, and it became possible to trap them in deep pools and kill them. This was done by piling earth, stones and logs into a pool where there was a *burus* and thereby burying it. The *burus* used to wave their head and long neck from side to side above the mud in their struggles: (this was imitated by a man waving his arm from side to side).

Our chief informant on the killing of the *burus* was a priest of Duta village named Chige Nime. A different version of one particular *buru* was given by Takhe Bdha, a man of Hang village. This version runs as follows: There was a *buru* in a pool near Hang. All the people gathered together, and omens were taken as to whether it should be destroyed. In Hang village were kept four magic plates of red metal called *mamla*, which had sharp edges. The *buru* bellowed, and the *mamla* left the village of their own accord, and cut it to pieces under water. The blood flowed up from below, and spreading over the surface of the water coloured it red. Then the people threw in earth, stones and logs, and made a mound over the place. Three of the original *mamla* have been destroyed or lost, but a small piece of one is preserved in Hang village, though no stranger is ever allowed to see it.

No one knows how many generations ago the *burus* were killed, but it was after the foundation of the present villages. Four are known to have been killed: the historical order of their destruction is remembered, and the sites are well known to everyone.

## (8) THE ACCOUNT OF TAMAR OF HANG

We again visited the valley late in 1946. During this visit we interrogated an old and much respected Apa Tani Priest, by name Tamar, and living in the great village of Hang. This man, who is well over seventy years of age, is somewhat crippled, never leaves his village, and has but little contact with men from outside villages. He was not questioned in 1945, and was not present during our inquiries. We established that the men we questioned in that year did not refer to him for information on our behalf.

His account of the *buru* tradition is given precisely as it was recorded:

Q. We have heard that there was once an animal here which you call the *buru*: can you tell us what it was like?

A. "It was like a big snake; it was as big as this." He then demonstrated that the girth was as much as a man could enclose in his arms: the gesture was several times repeated.

Q. What was its head like?

A. "It was like the head of a snake: it was broad and with a long snout. It had eyes deep set like a snake. There were three hard plates on the head, one on the top, and one on each side." This was demonstrated by Tamar placing a small rectangular mirror on the top and sides of his own head. He then stated that the *buru* "could use the plates to help it as it burrowed in the mud".

Q. What was its mouth like?

A. "It was like a snake's mouth."

Q. What were the teeth like?

A. "They were small."

Q. Do you know what the body was like?

A. "The *buru* was long: it had a long tail with flanges on the sides: they lay along it when resting, but were pushed out sideways when the beast was moving: it could twist its tail round and catch anything with it." The flanges were demonstrated by holding a piece of paper against a stick. We use the word "flange" for want of a better expression. Tamar described them as pieces fastened on the sides of the tail.

Q. Did it ever catch a man?

A. "A Dafla of the Tago clan, who was living in a settlement at the end of the valley was caught by the legs and pulled into the water. The *buru* did everything with its tail."

Q. How long was the tail?

A. Tamar measured along a bamboo lying near him, and showed that the tail was twice the length, approximately two and a half metres.

Q. What sort of legs did it have?

A. "It had no legs: the body was like a snake." Tamar then described and demonstrated that the tail flanges were grouped in two pairs, were about fifty centimetres long, and were as thick as a man's arm: he added they were used in burrowing. We got the impression that he was trying to convey the meaning that they were appendages, but not limbs in the true sense of the word. The question about the legs was accordingly repeated, and he again said there were none.

Q. If the *buru* had no legs, how did it move?

A. "It wriggled like a worm."

Q. What was the neck like?

A. "I do not know."

Q. Do you know what the skin is like?

A. "It was like a snake's skin."

Q. What colour was the *buru?*

A. He showed the colour of the cloth he was wearing, which was patterned in yellow, dark blue, white and red; and demonstrated that the colour was varied and had these colours in it. He was emphatic in showing the dark blue, and seemed to be trying to convey that the colour was blotched.

Q. Did the *buru* make any noise?

A. An imitation of a high-pitched bellow. "The noise was loud."

Q. Did the *buru* have a tongue?

A. "Yes, it had a tongue like a snake." He demonstrated a forked tongue with his fingers.

Q. Do you know what it ate?

A. "It lived on the mud."

Q. Then why did it kill the man of the Tago clan?

A. "He was out hunting, and found a young one asleep on the bank, which he speared. The mother killed him, and pulled his house into the water. This was at a place on the bank of the Kal River."

Q. How did the mother know he had killed her young one?

A. "She could tell who had killed it."

Q. How did the *buru* breed?

A. "The young ones were born alive. There were no eggs."

Q. How did it live? Did it always stay in the water?

A. "It used to come out on the banks in warm weather and lie curled up."

Q. Could it be seen when it was in the water?

A. "No, it always stayed under water."

Q. Was there only one *buru* or were they common?

A. "There were many of them."

Q. When the weather was cold and there was snow on the ground, did they come out of the water?

A. "No, they stayed deep down in the water and were not seen."

Q. How were they killed?

A. "By the mamla plates. These were round plates of red metal with sharp edges"—(this was demonstrated). "After killing the *buru* the plates killed a boy, and his mother broke them with a rice-pounder." He then told us there is a piece of one preserved in Hang village, and he mentioned the part of the village in which it is kept. We asked to see it, but were told it could not be shown to strangers.

Q. Do you know how long ago the *burus* were killed?

A. "No I do not know."

Q. By which clan were they killed?

A. "It was so long ago that we do not know. The Tago clan then here was not the same as the present one."

Q. What was its total length?

A. "It was as long as a *bobo* post": (these are poles from six to twelve metres long which are used ceremonially: and a *bobo* pole was the nearest long object to hand.)

Q. Were there many kinds of *buru*?

A. "No, there was only one kind."

Q. Do you know of any other animal like it?

A. "No, I know of no other like it."

Q. Have you heard of the crocodile of the Brahmaputra?

A. Tamar turned to a man standing by him. This man said he had been so far as the Brahmaputra River, and had seen a crocodile. Both he and Tamar stated, with emphatic shaking of their heads that the *buru* was not the same animal.

Q. Did the *buru* have any magical powers?

A. "No, it had no magical powers."

Q. Why did the people kill them?

A. "They were troublesome to them."

Q. Did the *burus* kill many men?

A. "No, only one man."

Q. Were they killed long after the Apa Tani people first came?

A. "They killed them quickly."

Q. Have any bones or teeth ever been found?

A. "No, they were killed so long ago that no bones or teeth are left now."

(9) THE SITES WHERE THE BURUS WERE FIRST KILLED

The four traditional sites where the *burus* were killed and buried are named according to their proximity to particular villages. We describe them in the order in which, according to tradition, the *burus* were killed.

*(a) The Hari site*

This is situated in the main valley, between the eastern edge of the swamp, and the central stream, on ground below the general level of that around it. The actual site is marked by a small pool, some three metres in diameter, and the only pool of its kind we found in the valley. It is among rice plots, and we were told that it is the only place in the valley from which it had never been possible to drain off the water sufficiently to permit of cultivation. The water is, in the dry season, about half a metre deep, with deep mud below it, and the site is clearly that of a deep pool in the ancient lake.

### (b) The Bela site

This is on the opposite side of the valley to, and half a mile distant from, the Hari site. It is also on low, cultivated ground, a few metres from the bank of an inlet of the main swamp. Our guide from Bela village was only able to point out the site as being somewhere within two rice plots covering an area of about a hundred square metres. He was careful to explain that he could not give it more exactly, as the little Shiya stream which used to mark the site had later been diverted to improve irrigation, and its former source was no longer apparent.

### (c) The Haja site

The traditional killing place near Haja village lies across the valley from the Bela site and like it is in low rice land close to the bank of a bay of the ancient swamp. No special feature seems to mark the site, but it was pointed out precisely and without hesitation.

### (d) The Hang site

Unlike the other three sites, this is at the south end of the plateau, but like them it is in low ground close to the edge of the swamp. We were taken straight to the place, which is marked precisely by a small circular raised patch of long grass and rushes, some twenty-five square metres in area in the middle of a rice plot. We naturally asked our guide, a man named Takhe Bdha of Hang village, why this little patch was left uncultivated: and in particular if it was an 'unlucky place' because a *buru* was said to be buried there. He replied: "No, it is not an unlucky place. At one time there was a big mound over the burial site, but the land was gradually levelled off for rice cultivation, and the small raised patch that is left marks what was once the top of the mound."

When we revisited the area in 1946 we again went to the burial sites. In three instances we had different guides, but were taken to the same sites.

## (10) *Buru remains*

The Apa Tanis told us in 1945 that they have never dug up or excavated any of the burial sites, but that seven generations back (the name of each succeeding descendant is known) a man named Takhe Saha of Hang village by chance found a skull of a *buru* in a corner of the central flat called *Chogho*. The skull was "like a pig's skull, with a long flat snout, slightly forked at the tip". This was illustrated by holding two fingers a little apart. Takhe Saha took the skull back to his house, but as he died soon afterwards, it was suspected of bringing him bad luck and was thrown away.

That the skull was that of a *buru* was of course an inference drawn by Takhe and his contemporaries from the traditional description of the beast. It is hard to believe that it could have been the skull of any existing animal known to the Apa Tanis, either domestic or wild, since tribal knowledge is unfailingly accurate in what are to primitive peoples, ordinary everyday objects.

### PART II: GENERAL COMMENTS

We wish to make it clear that in our analysis and discussion of the *buru* tradition, we are in no way concerned with its geological, climatic, or biological implications. We are considering it purely on its own merits, with a view to establishing how far it is interlarded with mythology, to what extent it savours of the fantastic, or contains any self-contradictory features; and to test, in so far as may be possible, the likely degree of accuracy of tribal memory.

## (1) THE RECORDING OF THE EVIDENCE

Throughout our investigations, every precaution was taken against influencing or prompting the replies given to our questions, leading questions being strictly avoided. The verbatim account of the interrogation of Tamar of Hang village (an instance of the technique followed throughout), shows that several times we were given a simple negative reply. The same occurred in 1945, as when we asked "Do you know anything of the young ones?" and were told "No, we do not." No sketch or diagram of what the *buru* might have looked like, or of any other animal was shown to the Apa Tanis, as we feared that to do so would inevitably formalise the beast in their minds and subconsciously influence their replies. Several interpreters were used, all of whose translations were checked and counter-checked, and they were made to repeat literally and word for word what was said to them. Our own ignorance of the Apa Tani language was naturally a severe handicap, but some of our informants themselves knew a little Assamese, and were able at times to give us their meaning direct. The free use of pantomime was of much help, and often gave the direct sense of what we were being told.

## (2) THE ACCOUNTS OF 1945 AND 1946 COMPARED

The main similarities and discrepancies between the accounts given us in 1945 and that given by Tamar in 1946 are self-evident, and we do not propose to discuss them in detail. There are, however, a few points which call for comment. (i) *The description:* The main discrepancy is in the contradictory statements regarding the limbs, one version describes the limbs, and the other denies their existence. But although Tamar said there were no limbs, he was apparently trying to explain that there were no limbs as he understood the term. His reference to flanges of the thickness of a man's arm, which were used in burrowing, and were in pairs is very reminiscent of the accounts given by other men of short limbs.

Tamar was quite obviously thinking of a *buru* in terms of a snake, with which he compared it whenever possible. On the other hand, he made it clear that the animal was not a snake, and his account of the habits could hardly have derived from any known snake. The other informants differed from him in that they seemed to be thinking of the *buru* purely as a distinct type of animal and not in terms of any known to them. It is noteworthy that comparisons were never made with a crocodile.

## (3) THE BURU AND APA TANI MYTHOLOGY

Neither Dr. Haimendorf (in his unpublished notes) nor ourselves have been able to discover any reference in Apa Tani mythology to any animal with outstanding or profound religious significance. Indeed, when Dr. Haimendorf left the plateau in 1945 after some months of study of tribal culture, he was quite unaware of the *buru* tradition. He was merely told that the swamp was once the home of "snakes and monsters", and he recorded the killing of one such monster by a magic plate of metal. But he did not pursue this line of inquiry, nor did he gain the impression that these "monsters" played any important role in Apa Tani mythology or religion.

## (4) THE ATTITUDE OF OUR INFORMANTS

Our informants were clearly surprised that we should take so much interest in what was, to them, a matter of no practical importance at all. We were particularly struck by the completely matter of fact manner in which the whole story was retailed. At no time was the *buru* invested with any magical powers, or given any religious significance. When we visited the Hari burial site, we were told that the pool was the home of a "Ui" or spirit, but it was also explained, in

3

reply to our question, that its semi-sacred significance is in no way connected with a *buru* having been killed there.

A parallel instance is that of the Hang site, where as already recorded, the grassy patch is not uncultivated because of its traditional associations. Again, the homely tale of the collapse of the house at Duta Lapang does not imply any direct connection with the creature, beyond its presence. The only clear touch of mythology is in the story of the killing of the Hang *buru* by the *mamla*. The plates were, however, the agency responsible for its death, and other recorded stories, such as that of their having killed a boy, make it clear that they did not require a *buru* to bring out the magical properties, which were displayed under other conditions. The significance of the *mamla* legend is not easy to assess, without further material, but it would seem to have had some foundation since a small piece of one plate is preserved, although not allowed to be shown: a very frequent practice among tribes of this region where their sacred relics are concerned.

The *mamla* strongly suggests former possession by the Apa Tanis of the disc-knife or *Chakram*, particularly since this weapon was propelled by throwing. We have not, however, been able to discover if the *chakram* was formerly used in this region. It is unknown at the present day in either Assam or the surrounding region. A particularly realistic touch is given to this legend by the statement, several times repeated, that after the *buru* killed by the *mamla* was cut "its blood flowed up and coloured the top of the water red". There is a significant absence from any of the accounts of mention of the use of swords, iron-tipped arrows, and spears, which are the present-day weapons of the Apa Tanis: such weapons would be useless for killing aquatic animals.

The whole attitude of the Apa Tanis towards the *buru* may be paraphrased: "When our forefathers first came, there was a great beast in the lake. It was quite new to them, and

# LIST OF ILLUSTRATIONS

Tamar of Hang, an Apa Tani priest, gives a vivid description of the Buru.

A view over part of the Apa Tani plateau, now rice fields,
but once a primeval swamp.

Scene in Seidjhosa Camp. Izzard in foreground.

Izzard beside a typical long Dafla house. These hold several families, often totaling a few hundred souls.

A scene in an Apa Tani village.

Tapook the Magnificent, planner of many little villainies, who heartily distrusted the camera.

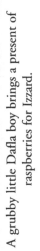

A grubby little Dafla boy brings a present of raspberries for Izzard.

Pupils and principal of the Rilo Typing School. Daflas can neither read nor write, but they never tired of playing with the typewriter.

Eldest son and daughter of the Headman of Rilo village.

Frank drinking Dafla beer at the house of Dedum, Headman of Rilo.

A bull Mithan in the jungle.

A Dafla in Rilo village making iron arrow heads and shaping them. The barb is then covered with poison.

A Sulung. This tribe is more primitive than the Dafla, but they are pleasanter to deal with.

Sulungs: Pingling and his baby girl Mohai leave on an expedition.

Making bamboo ladders for the Buru swamp. They are being made in thick jungle on the edge of the swamp. Both dim-dams and leeches were bad here.

Carrying the bamboo ladders into the swamp. The reeds met overhead, and in boggy ground the going was heavy.

A traditional killing place of the Buru, now a small pool in the rice fields, near the village of Hari.

Headman Thai, wearing his red coat of office, arrives in camp with
Tagora, interpreter and arch-cadger.

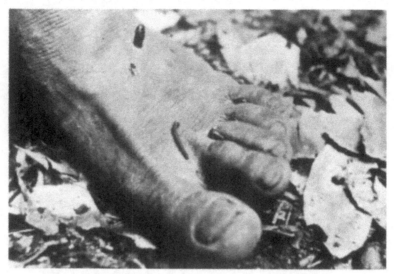

On the march porters with bare feet were greatly troubled by leeches.
Here a porter has stopped with leeches between toes and on instep.

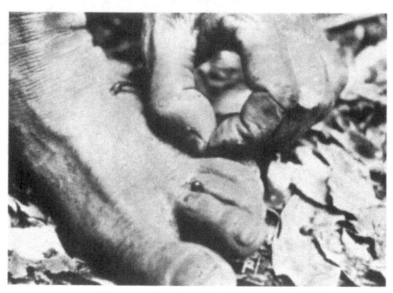

The same foot as in the above picture.
The porter removes a leech from between his toes.

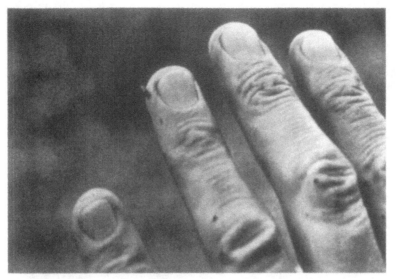

A dim-dam on Frank's hand, which shows the scars of former bites.
These bites are maddeningly irritating and can cause acute swelling.

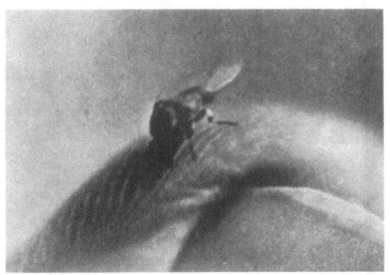

A magnified picture of a dim-dam at work on Frank's hand.

Lenko, a West Dafla village, had a great variety of sacrificial posts and emblems. Symbols represent birds, beasts, and other objects of worship.

was a nuisance. As the lake was drained, it became possible to kill the beasts."

Much in the same way the Maoris have told of the great Moas of New Zealand.

## (5) INFLUENCES FROM OUTSIDE SOURCES

Firstly, we have the positive statement that the *buru* was quite new to the tribe when they reached the valley. We asked about this several times, and were given the same reply.

Secondly, as we shall consider below, all comparisons were made with other animals found in and around the valley. We were careful to inquire directly if the Apa Tanis had heard of any other animal like the *buru*, either in the Plains or elsewhere, and received a completely negative reply. We stress again the remarkable isolation of the tribe: this was vividly brought home to us in 1945 when a few leading men accompanied us to the Plains on our return journey, and were completely dumbfounded on seeing men riding on ponies.

Although they know of the existence of the crocodile, they definitely do not link the *buru* with it, and no comparisons were made with it. Such comparisons would hardly have been avoided if the tradition had been from a crocodile.

## (6) THE EVIDENCE OF THE BURIAL SITES

The burial sites have a close general similarity with one another, and they accord well with the accounts of how the *buru* was trapped or isolated in deep pools left by the receding water. All of them are in low ground relative to the general level of the swamp, ground such as well might have contained deep pools. This is true of the Hari site in particular, which is pointed out as the only place in the cultivated area which the Apa Tanis have been unable to drain. With the exception of this site, all are very similarly situated, a few metres out from the high bank, and in branches or inlets of the main swamp—precisely the type of place in which a large aquatic animal could be 'cornered' and dispatched by men standing on the high bank above it. It may not be without significance that the Hang site, said to mark the killing of the last *buru*, should also preserve traces of a traditional mound over the spot.

### (7) THE TRADITION AND TRIBAL MEMORY

It seems at first sight highly improbable that a primitive tribe such as the Apa Tanis living under neolithic conditions, should have preserved, wholly by verbal tradition, an account so detailed and so full of almost trivial features. But, all who have made direct contact with primitive people, ignorant of the written word, have been struck by the extraordinary accuracy of tribal memory and the vividness of tradition: and comparison with verbal traditions of other peoples in all countries, provides many parallels with the one we are considering.

### (8) THE METHOD OF DESCRIPTION

An important consideration is the manner in which the account was given. Four methods were employed by the tellers: (i) gesture; (ii) imitation; (iii) comparison; and (iv) direct description.

(i) Gestures were used to give all measurements, which, as recorded, were mainly in terms of a man's limbs. Thus, the girth was as much as a man could enclose in his arms; the breadth over the back was equal to a man's arm outstretched, plus the width of his body; the neck was the length of a man's arm; the legs were the length of a man's forearm; the tail was the length of a man's arm outstretched and across his body to the elbow of the other arm; the depth of water required by a *buru* to live in was more than the height of a man. Each of these items was invariably accompanied by the appropriate descriptive gesture. This simple comparative method of stating measurements is necessarily standard among peoples with no system of units. Naturally enough they are only an approximation, but the measurements as given us in 1945 total up to a perfectly reasonably proportioned animal. The total length of four metres was the first given, the others being shown later, and all were repeated more than once. No actual figure was given for the body length, but on the basis of the above figures we have an overall length of four metres, a head and neck of one metre, and a tail of one and a half metres; leaving one and a half metres for the body—not by any means an unreasonable proportion. At the same time it must not be forgotten that the simple system of measurements known to the Apa Tanis would be likely to formalise their tradition of the proportions, since they were handed down always in the terms of a man's body. In a similar way Tamar was presumably influenced in his version of the length by his comparison with a *bobo* pole—the nearest available object.

(ii) Imitation was used to convey the bellowing noise, the drawing in and stretching out of the neck, and the waving of the head from side to side.

(iii) Comparisons were given wherever possible, mainly in respect of local animals, and were carefully selected. For instance, a mole's forelimbs were used to describe stumpy limbs or flippers. Similarly, the teeth were flat, and so like those of a man, with tushes like a boar. The skin was like that of a fish; the skull resembled that of a pig with a long snout. The skull of a pig is of course long-snouted, and the one picked up might have been that of a pig. But pigs are one of the main domestic animals of the Apa Tanis and Daflas, and the skulls of wild pigs killed are very commonly kept in their houses; so that a pig's skull is a common everyday object recognisable at a glance to all members of these tribes. It therefore seems inconceivable that Takhe Saha and his friends would not have known a pig's skull when they saw it.

The comparison of the skull picked up with that of a pig thus gives considerable emphasis to the traditional length of the *buru's* snout, and the same was emphasised although in a different way, by Tamar in 1946. For the colour, the nearest objects held to be similar were used: by one informant our own blue drinking cups, and by Tamar his own cloth. Although comparisons were so freely used, there was no suggestion of an attempt to describe a composite animal. Our informants never tried to show that the *buru* was a fish with the head of a pig, and the teeth of a man; and they were quite clear that they looked on their traditional beast as quite distinct from any present-day animal.

(iv) Direct description was used when direct comparison was difficult, and the informant invariably demonstrated his meaning with the aid of material objects. For instance, to explain the short blunt spines, the tips of palm fibre on a rain cloak were used, with the added explanation that the spines of the *buru* were thicker and blunter. To demonstrate the tail flanges, leaves were nipped to shape, and placed along the sides of a stick laid on the ground: while to show the head plates Tamar placed a rectangular object on his own head.

It is noteworthy that in describing the habits, no comparisons with other animals were ever made.

Thus, every detail of the appearance and habits is recorded in essentially simple terms, such as are easily remembered and easily passed on. Such a technique has obvious limitations and scope for stylisation, but we felt throughout that we were given the story precisely as it had been handed down to each successive generation by the old men of the community.

In estimating the weight to be given to the tradition, the complete absence of any knowledge of writing, drawing, or carving, such as would probably have standardised the *buru*, must be borne in mind. It may well be asked why a primitive tribe such as the Apa Tanis should have taken the trouble to preserve the *buru* tradition in such detail. Here again, it is necessary to bear in mind the small compass and extreme narrowness of their existence throughout centuries: so that what would to our world be a triviality, would to them be a major event. They can have had but few landmarks in their recent history, and it would be but natural for a unique episode such as the killing of the *buru* to have been handed down and remembered in detail.

## PART III. THE TRADITIONAL COMPARED WITH THE MYTHS OF LEGENDARY MONSTERS

### (a) *Considered as a possible dragon myth*

The common features of the dragon myth are summarised in an appendix to this paper (Appendix). The dragon is of its very nature a symbol, and not a legendary monster in the real meaning of the term. It is the product of blending and reblending of ideas among peoples with a relatively high level of civilisation. Like all such myths it is a response to needs; and for a dragon to be shorn of all its magical and symbolical qualities, and all the fantastic features of its essentially composite anatomy, and for a "reasonable" form and natural habits to be substituted, would be unique among civilised peoples, and would be utterly out of tune with the whole nature of the myth. For a people such as the Apa Tani tribe, with a culture far lower than any people known to possess the dragon, even to know it would be remarkable enough: for them to *transform* it into a tradition such as that of the *buru* would, in our opinion be virtually impossible, and would involve a religious and mythological background comparable with a high civilisation.

### (b) *The tradition relative to the mythology of neighbouring tribes*

Knowledge of all the tribes inhabiting the Assam Himalayas is still lamentably small, but so far nothing has come to light of any comparable tradition among Daflas, Abors, or

Mishmis, who form the main cultural elements of the population. The *buru* tradition has certainly no parallel in the Assam-Burma Frontier. Small lakes and pools are scattered about the region, and are invariably regarded as the homes of spirits: but there is no case known where any legend at all comparable with that of the *buru* exists.

If we also take into account the complete absence of similar areas to the Apa Tani plateau in this region, we can rule out any likelihood of the people having brought the tradition with them and reapplied it to their present area. There is also their own statement that the *buru* was new to them when they reached the lake.

Lacustrine monsters are no more associated with the general run of legendary beliefs among mountain peoples than are sea-serpents. The *buru* is, for the Apa Tanis, a tradition connected with the valley in which they live and nowhere else. The Daflas of the surrounding region also know of the tradition and associate it with the Apa Tani plateau only. We asked the headman of a Dafla village two days' march from the nearest Apa Tani village if he had ever heard of an animal known as a *buru*. He replied "that is the animal which once caused such trouble among the Apa Tanis in their country that they had to get special plates from their gods with which to kill it". The same man stated that he had never been to the valley.

### (c) *The buru and other traditional or legendary monsters*

As we have endeavoured to show, it is quite impossible for the Apa Tanis to have had any preconceived ideas of the appearance of any of the great reptiles, either extinct or recent, except the crocodile. In many cases stories of legendary monsters have been proved to be based on the finding of prehistoric remains.

Dr. Tindell Hopwood has stressed this in a private letter: "The German tales of the Lindwurm, and the various Dragon Caves are woven round cave deposits containing remains of the cave bear and other large animals. Indeed, in so far as Europe is concerned I have the strong impression that the legends are attempts to explain the presence of the bones rather than memories of the animals themselves." It may, therefore, be argued that the entire *buru* tradition is based on the finding of an unknown type of skull in the swamp. But were, for instance, a strange skull to be found in a swamp in Europe, local opinion would, in all probability, invest it with the form of some beast of which the local inhabitants had some previous knowledge, either from popular literature, or from a visit to a museum: it would, in short, be described in terms of something already known to the discoverers, and were news of the discovery to be prevented from spreading, we can imagine how a legend and tradition could grow up around it.

But, if we are to make any attempt at assessing the pros and cons of the *buru* tradition, we are bound to consider it *in its setting*, and in relationship to the tribe responsible for it: to consider its implications apart from attendant circumstances and divorced from the Apa Tanis would be a manifest absurdity. We are quite unable to envisage a primitive people living culturally in the neolithic period, weaving the entire tradition, not excluding the burial sites, round a single unknown skull, and developing from their own imagination the form and habits of the beast.

We are therefore left with three possibilities:

(i) The Apa Tanis evolved from their imagination, a tradition of an animal in their lake, which, by sheer coincidence, has no fantastic features when considered in comparison with the form and habits of large aquatic reptiles both recent and extinct.

(ii) Secondly, it may be assumed that the tradition is based on a legend of a purely mythical monster (or dragon) derived from other sources, and applied to the lake: this legendary monster having been, in the course of generations shorn of literally all its magical attributes, and having become entirely rationalised and invested with a form and history quite different from those of any other known legendary monster in Asia.

(iii) Thirdly, we are left with the explanation that when describing the *buru* the Apa Tanis were telling of an animal their ancestors actually saw, and the form and habits of which have been passed down to our own times.

### SUMMARY AND CONCLUSIONS

(i) The Apa Tani tribe have a remarkable tradition of a great aquatic reptile which formerly inhabited the lake on the fringe of which they have their home. To this animal they have given the name of *buru*.

(ii) This tradition avoids in a striking manner endowing the animal with any magical associations or powers.

(iii) The tradition gives a detailed account of both form and habits of the *buru*, and of the manner of its final extinction.

(iv) There is no means whereby the Apa Tani tribe can have known of the present or former existence of aquatic reptiles except the crocodile.

(v) They are able to show the exact sites where four of the animals are said to have been killed and buried. Unfortunately our knowledge of the geology and climatic history of this region of the Himalayas is extremely poor, and none of the area concerned has ever been geologically surveyed. It is therefore impossible to consider the *buru* tradition in association with the history of its environment, and we have confined ourselves entirely to its historical aspect as a tradition of the tribe.

However convinced we ourselves may be of its truth, it is clearly impossible to regard the tradition as historical fact unless confirmatory evidence of a more concrete nature can be produced. The excavation of the burial sites is no easy task: and practical difficulties of all kinds are very real.

*The Dragon Myth*

The dragon myth is of very great complexity, and has, in the words of Sir Grafton Elliot Smith "evolved along with civilisation itself". It is a myth of civilised peoples only: and although it occurs in every civilisation of the past in Europe, Asia, Africa and America, there is no known instance of a culturally primitive people, practising a simple form of animistic religion, possessing the myth. The dragon is essentially associated with the myths of peoples of high cultural level, and is altogether out of place in a modern neolithic culture.

The dragon is anatomically a purely composite animal, whose form is independent of scientific reality, and is invariably fantastic with the head of an eagle, and the hindparts of a lion (Egypt), the head of an elephant and the hindparts of a fish (India), and so on. The possession of supernatural powers is a *sine qua non* of the dragon myth wherever it occurs. Indeed, the supernatural powers of the dragon are its whole essence, the external form merely the symbol of its powers. An invariable attribute is the control of rain and water in general: it may be a symbol of either good or evil.

# CHAPTER III

# The Burus of Rilo Valley

THE SECOND DOCUMENT WAS ENCLOSED IN A SEPARATE sealed envelope which bore the inscription: "Not to be opened until the first account is read."

It ran as follows:

In February 1947 I visited an area of the Outer Himalayas, some fifty miles distant (as the crow flies) from the Apa Tani valley, where the tradition of the monster exists.

The country is essentially similar to the region surrounding that valley, and consists of an endless series of ranges, mounting gradually upwards to the north, to the Great Himalayan Range. It is exceedingly little known, and has been visited by only one survey party, and political officers have made occasional brief tours for administrative purposes. Otherwise it is virtually unexplored. The sole inhabitants are a branch of the Dafla tribe who extend over a great stretch of country. It is connected with the plains by a few narrow paths over the ranges, and is virtually impenetrable during the rainy season.

The first six ranges, which run up to six thousand feet are covered with thick forest, and are very thinly inhabited. It is five or six days' stiff marching to reach the thickly populated interior.

While I was going through this jungle region, I asked some Daflas in the course of casual conversation if they had ever heard of an animal called a buru. They recognised the name at once, and told me it was an animal of a swamp ahead of us.

I visited this area on 6th February. It is a great flat area, shut in some two thousand feet above sea-level. The total area I guessed at upwards of three square miles. The greater part of it is dry, and is of sandy silt; it struck me at once that it must be a silted up lake or swamp. It has never before been visited by Europeans. There is a small Dafla village at one corner of the flat area: and I told the inhabitants that I had come to ask about an animal called a buru. The villagers at once pointed to a corner of the great flat area, and I learnt that this was still impassable swamp, and that here the buru STILL LIVED.

I replied that such a thing was impossible, and that the animal was a spirit and not a real beast at all. The people asked why and laughed openly at me.

I was taken to a remote corner of the area, and from a hill overlooking it I could see, some seven hundred yards below me, a swamp, perhaps three thousand yards in extent, and with, even at the height of the dry weather, pools of water. I was given the following account of the buru . . .

During the rainy season, the swamp quickly floods to become a large lake; and when the water rises large animals appear from the swamp. They live under water, and every now and again they come up above the surface. When one of them comes up there is a great disturbance and splashing, and the beast comes straight up out of the water, stays for a few moments only, and then disappears down again. Sometimes eight or ten of them are seen up at the same time, and it is believed that there are many in the swamp. They are much bigger than a man, and are bulky animals the same shape and size as the tame bison. They have small horns, but they point backwards instead of sideways like those of a bison. Like the bison they are coloured black and white. They are never seen very clearly as they only come up for a few moments, and it is not possible to get nearer to the swamp than the surrounding hills. They are most often seen when the sun is bright. They are seen from about May to September, when the swamp is a lake. In the dry season, when the lake becomes a marsh, they go down below the swamp and are never seen. "If you come here in the rainy season you are sure to see them" . . .

The above is, of course, a composite account, and is the sum total of the information I was able to get. For that reason it needs certain qualification. (i) I checked every statement by asking different individuals on different occasions. (ii) The colour was invariably given as black and white. (iii) I asked again and again if it was large or small, and about the shape. I was invariably told that "they are like our tame bison". (iv) The statements that they are most often seen when the sun is bright, that they come out of the water for a few moments only, that they are horned, and that they are only seen in summer, were entirely volunteered.

I should add that the tame Bison (Mithan) are the centre of Dafla economic life: and that any large black and white animal would *ipso facto* be compared with them.

While I was in the village there were about fifty people present: men, women and children. I asked the headman how many of those present had seen a buru. He waved his arm to indicate the whole village, and added that they see them every time they go to work in the fields overlooking the swamp during the summer months.

I also made a special point later on of inquiring in the other villages of this part of the hills. Everywhere I was given the same story: "There are burus in the swamp at Rilo." In several villages I met people who had visited this area during the summer months. They all told me that they had seen burus when they were there, and all gave the same account.

A few days after my return from the hills I met a Dafla living on the plains. I asked him casually if he knew of an animal called a buru. He at once said that he did, and they were found at a place called Rilo where he himself used to live. This man was quite unaware that I had been there, and I did not let on that I knew the place until I had listened to his account. Once more I was given precisely the same brief account: "the burus are large animals, which only appear when the marsh becomes a lake in the summer". He stated that they are seen when they come up out of the water for a few moments. The head is like that of a bison, but he added that: "it has a longer nose, more like that of the ponies kept near here by the Nepalis". He has seen about three at the same time. In order to try and trap him, I asked what its teeth are like, and if it is hairy. He replied: "How can I know since we only see them from afar off." He added that he has only seen them on sunny days, and he thought they never appeared in dull weather.

At first sight it appears beyond belief that a great aquatic beast could exist, even in this remote region, without so much as a hint of its existence having reached the outside world. But, if we consider the attendant circumstances, I think it can be shown that such a thing is quite feasible (excluding the biological aspect). (i) I have already stated that the area has only been visited four or five times in all, and then for a few weeks only, during the dry season. No Government Officer except myself has ever seen the Rilo swamp. No plainsman has ever thought of visiting these hills.

The Dafla tribe is of uncertain origin: but they have no affinities, cultural, or linguistic, with the plains people. Furthermore they are a people of an exceedingly primitive outlook: their religion, social organisation, etc. are very primitive indeed—more so than among any tribal people I have yet encountered. Their world is bound by the Great Himalayan Range on the north, and the Brahamaputra to the south.

(ii) The presence of a great animal in a swamp is no more remarkable to the Daflas than is the Blind Dolphin of the Brahamaputra to the plains people of Assam.

Far from being an object of wonder, the buru is an animal of no consequence whatsoever. They cannot get near it or kill it: it is of no use to them as food, it does not interfere in their lives. My repeated questionings were met with tolerant amusement. The Daflas made it clear that they thought me a little mad for being interested in such a trivial matter. Had I not happened to mention it, it is remotely unlikely that they would ever have referred to it at all. For all they knew there are innumerable swamps and lakes in the outer world with countless burus inhabiting them.

The following points emerge from the above. (i) From the nature of its habitat, the beast must be vegetarian. (ii) Like all existing swamp reptiles it hibernates. (iii) All informants agreed that when it is seen it comes vertically out of the water with much splashing, showing its head and part of the body. There is no suggestion that it travels along with its head out of the water. This seems most peculiar, and leads one to wonder just how it can propel itself. (iv) The beast is seen from a considerable distance only, and then only rather vaguely. The fact that under such circumstances it can be described as having a snout and a head the size of a bison, suggests an animal of no mean size. Since the shape of the head suggests a bison to the Daflas I think it may well be regarded automatically as being horned. The more so since all the few large animals known to the Daflas are horned or antlered or tusked. On the other hand, all informants were positive that it is horned. (v) The statement that they are most often seen when the sun is bright suggests a slow, sluggish beast which is only activated by direct warmth of the sun.

An extraordinary feature of the story is that the beast could survive in such a relatively minute space. But the area in which it is now said to live was once a swamp of about three square miles, which has presumably been silted up by slow stages, and of which enough still remains to support it.

C. R. STONOR.

CHAPTER IV

# Preparations

BY THE TIME I HAD TYPED OUT THE TWO ACCOUNTS AND SENT them to the *Daily Mail*, the eagerly awaited cable arrived from London. As I had thought it must be it was favourable, enthusiastic. Translated from the jargon of cablese it read: "Yes, for pity's sake press on with expedition. Tell Stonor we'll finance him to the hilt. Possibilities are enormous." I had cleared my major obstacle; I could keep faith with Stonor. I was free of the shackles; from that moment on I was dedicated to the hunt for the buru.

But although we could now start on a firm financial footing, and although I had been granted all the time I required, the technical difficulties of launching the expedition were only just beginning.

In the first place, Rilo swamp lies in the heart of the Balipara Frontier Tract. Tribes round Rilo were considered friendly; they were known to be truculent in the country to the north, reaching to the closed Tibetan frontier, where reputedly stand sentinels still wearing chain mail. None can enter a Frontier Tribal Area in India without first obtaining permission from the Government. This permission is rarely granted, and rightly so, for a single rash act by an inexperienced man can so unsettle the tribes that their subsequent pacification may become a costly business lasting some years. This, of course, hardly applied to Stonor as an experienced Government servant, but nevertheless he too would have to seek official sanction. It so happened that when this matter first became urgent Sir Akbar Hydari, Governor of Assam, who would have to make the final decision, was away from Shillong on tour.

Two other important questions could only be answered following the return of Sir Akbar. In the first place Stonor himself would have to ask for a generous allowance of time away from his desk in Shillong. It could well be argued that no time spent in a little known tribal area would be wasted for him. He could utilise the hunt for the buru in order to make a much needed detailed survey of agricultural conditions among the Daflas. But there was always a possibility that he might be required for some more urgent task.

In the second place we had still not solved our main worry, which was porters. We were about to attempt something never normally done; an excursion into mountain-jungle country during the rainy season. At that time mountain streams become unfordable torrents; precipitous paths unscalable owing to a greasy coating of slime. Every yard of the route and each square foot of every camp site crawls with leeches. Aware of the prize, we ourselves might face such conditions; but we should have great difficulty in getting the porters to face them. We could not rely on casual Dafla labour. The Daflas are notorious as the most feckless and indolent of all the frontier tribes of Assam. We should need at least a stiffening of regular Gurkha porters, and these we could not obtain without Sir Akbar's help.

All these facts Stonor communicated to me by letter as we both waited anxiously for Sir Akbar's return. It would still not have suprised me in the least if the whole thing had fallen through. It had seemed too good to be true from the beginning. It had started when an inconspicuous nugget of news had been accidentally kicked in the path of a Foreign Correspondent. I had picked up the nugget and scratched the surface. Surely it was too much to expect that the nugget should prove to be pure gold?

But once more our luck held. Stonor's next letter brought the best possible news. Sir Akbar Hydari had not only given his official sanction to the trip; he had entered enthusiastically into the spirit of the thing. We were to draw as many

Gurkhas as we wanted from his own Porter Corps. Hard on the heels of this information came an additional cause for congratulation. Earl Mountbatten of Burma, then Governor-General of India, returning from Rangoon, stopped off in Assam to pay a short visit to Shillong as guest of Sir Akbar. News of the impending hunt for the buru was duly communicated to him. Stonor was produced; Earl Mountbatten followed his story with the keenest possible interest; finally he cheerfully agreed to become the Patron of the party.

At that stage we could hardly have wished for more; we had all the time we wanted to work in; all the money we should need; the highest official blessings. Then came the next hurdle. For some time we had been worried about the question of getting adequate photographic proof. Both Stonor and I were still anxious to trim down stores and equipment to the minimum, but neither of us had any real working experience of highly specialised cameras fitted with telephoto lenses. The *Daily Mail* attitude was that they were prepared to take a sporting chance on the buru not being there, but, were we to discover it, they wanted the fullest possible photographic coverage, both still pictures and a cinema film. Quite understandably, they did not want us merely to peck at the "story" and then leave it to someone else to scoop the pool. They were prepared to fly a professional camera-man out from London but they were dubious about his ability to fly from a London March and acclimatise himself rapidly enough to India to be of any use in summer jungle conditions. Could we recruit someone locally? I passed on this information to Stonor and back came a gloomy reply that while he appreciated the London view we must, above all watch the weight question. An additional European could entail anything up to thirty extra porters, and beyond a certain number, porters were simply not available no matter how much money we offered. However, there seemed to be nothing else for it. The problem, then, was where to find a suitable man? Stonor, "exiled" in Shillong could make no suggestion, and I was at my wit's end where to turn, when quite by chance I bumped into Frank Hodgkinson. Frank had started his career with the Indian Army but had later devoted himself to camera work with expeditions which had probed into strange places in many parts of the East.

He already had every type of camera we should require and could use them expertly. In addition he was immensely strong, with a chest like a Master at Arms. It scarcely seemed possible that he could be available at such short notice. But Frank took one look at the Stonor correspondence and the two reports on the buru, and announced at once that we could count him in. Thus the party was made up.

We were past the main obstacles, all that remained was a great deal of routine work, the collection of stores, equipment and special gear such as the collapsible boats. This was pleasurable work; all part of the game, and now that we were entitled to ask help from professionals and experts we met with assistance on every hand.

Brigadier Heany, Director-General of the Survey of India, provided us with aerial photographs and ¼-inch maps, with the warning that we should not rely too much on contour form lines, routes or place names as much of the data was purely speculative.

The Himalayan Club generously lent us all the lightweight tents we should require.

Two five-man air-sea rescue type collapsible rubber dinghies were found for us in Calcutta by Darrel MacMahon, the *Daily Mail* representative there.

We searched the world by cable for the right type of film for Frank's cameras, ran them to earth in the U.S.A. and arranged for their dispatch to us.

Everything went smoothly; our list of kit was complete down to such last minute items as the tobacco ration and the rum bottles, and then the disaster occurred which nearly put me right out of the Buru expedition.

I was cantering into the dawn across the mud flats on the far side of Old Delhi when suddenly my horse plunged with his forefeet into a hole and turned right over. In no time at all I was sitting in a splintered tamarisk bush nursing a broken collar-bone, three cracked ribs and a badly wrenched shoulder. That was on Sunday, March 21st; on Thursday the 25th I was due to leave Delhi for Calcutta and Shillong!

Of the immediate results of the accident all I remember is a painful walk of a mile back to the road, hugging my elbow and supported by my wife; a ride in a borrowed car to Colonel Taylor, the Governor-General's surgeon; a morphia-deadened sensation as Taylor put his knee between my shoulders, and forced them back to get the broken bone in place. At length I came to in bed at home, trussed in a straight jacket like a lunatic. Then I pondered ruefully on the prospects for my hunt for the buru. At first I felt like damning the consequences, and carrying on the pro-gramme as previously arranged. But Taylor said this would be madness; no bone could knit by will power alone. He was also quite right when he said that as the days passed I should feel less and less like heroics. I cabled Stonor informing him of the accident and my determination to go through with the expedition. All I asked was for him to let me know if there was likely to be any postponement, as I should welcome the chance of an extra day or two in bed. But Stonor was pitiless. His cable in reply began: "Have no repeat no sympathy." He then suggested that instead of coming to Shillong I should join him at Lokra, our jumping off point, on 4th April. This meant that, regretfully, I had to decline Sir Akbar Hydari's invitation to spend a few days at Government House, Shillong, but it did give me an extra ten day's grace, and that, I felt, would be sufficient. Stonor would carry out the original programme and leave Shillong on 1st April. "That auspicious date," he said, "must not be abandoned!" The next hours passed as slowly, and perversely the next days as quickly, as any I remember.

To begin with my ribs were so painful that I could not lie longer than two hours in the same position without getting on my feet and walking round the room. But no sooner was I on my feet than the collar-bone and shoulder began aching and I had to lie down again. Thus the hours seemed interminable. But the days slipped by with alarming rapidity, and the end of the first week arrived with no real improvement in my condition. On the following Thursday, the 1st April, still feeling weak and shaky I again went to Taylor's surgery, and emerged tightly swathed in Elastoplast. This was an uncomfortable though first-class running repair and Taylor felt that I would do.

Now, we could no longer afford to waste time; but a new set of complications was upon us. A mass of stores, including the boats and the tents, had assembled at Calcutta. My first emergency plan after the accident had been to send Darrel MacMahon to escort the gear by rail as far as Gauhati, Assam, where we should join him on Saturday, 3rd April. We could then travel overnight to Lokra which we should reach on the following morning. We then learned that the consignment of films which were being flown from America would not arrive until the night of Friday the 2nd, which meant that we could not possibly keep the Gauhati rendezvous. Simultaneously came a *cri de coeur* from Stonor that unless we could reach Lokra on Sunday, 4th April, he would have a mutiny of the Dafla porters on his hands. To appease Stonor I therefore cabled Darrel to start a day earlier, and go right through to Lokra; the baggage which he brought with him should at least keep the porters quiet. By an unfortunate mischance this cable never arrived.

Frank Hodgkinson and I booked our air passages from Delhi to Calcutta for Saturday the 3rd.

# CHAPTER V

# Delhi–Lokra

THAT SATURDAY THE TEMPERATURE SAILED UP TO NEARLY 100 degrees in the shade. It seemed incredible that barely two weeks before we had been hunting. Our plane was due to leave at two in the afternoon, and in the heat of high noon I was driven to Palam airfield outside Delhi in a private car, which carefully avoided the bumps and potholes. It was the jolting in omnibuses and airplanes I feared more than the march ahead of us.

At Palam, where I joined up with Frank, we were once more overcome with anxiety. The plane which was to take us to Calcutta sat baking in the sun with one engine out of action; the duty engineer was nowhere to be found, and it looked suspiciously like no flight that day! No flight meant that we should miss the air connection arranged for us from Calcutta to Gauhati on the following morning. Possibly the implacable Stonor would have his mutiny after all! However, after a seemingly interminable delay we were suddenly invited to "enplane". It was more than a surprise, it was scarcely believable. We arrived two hours late in Calcutta. A long time before, Alex Campbell, also of the *Daily Mail*, who was to meet us with last-minute news of the stores, had rung up the airfield, had been cheerily told the Delhi plane was "in" and there was no one of our names on it. Thus when we reached Spence's Hotel there was somewhat naturally no Alex.

After the elations and depressions of the day, there was one thing we both needed, and that was a stiff drink, but it proved one of the newly instituted "drinkless" days in Calcutta, and all the hotel could offer was ginger-beer. An indication of my helplessness at that stage was that while I was able to climb into a bath and wash myself, I could not for the life of me get out of it. Finally, I had to be hoisted bodily to my feet by the burly Frank. It was some time before Alex came home, but thinking of everything as he always did he had brought with him a bottle of brandy. Over this we sat through the sticky, humid night until two in the morning, discussing future plans and the coming trip. It turned out that none of my cables sent during that week had reached either Campbell or Darrel MacMahon; thus Darrel would have gone no further than Gauhati. Neither Frank nor I dared to think of Stonor's predicament!

We were up again at four, and at five-thirty we were standing on the airfield waiting for the Gauhati plane. Calcutta, with its moist, decayed air of dilapidation, its filthy streets and its scaling pink and primrose plaster, has always had a morbid fascination for me, but that day I was glad to leave it. This was the beginning of the journey proper. Already civilisation, with its built-up areas, towns, villages, the intense cultivation of the plains, the cluttered river traffic of the Brahmaputra, was slipping rapidly away beneath us. We were headed towards limitless, sombre forests, high mountains, unknown country, little trodden paths. That glorious morning our hearts beat strongly and our hopes ran high.

We landed safely on the narrow jungle clearing which is the Gauhati air-strip. Soon we were swaying and bumping in a battered old bus towards the railway station. Miniature, fawn-coloured cattle moved lazily out of our path as we bore down upon them, our driver honking furiously on an ancient bulb horn. In contrast to Delhi, with its surrounding desolate, sun-scorched plains, dotted with arid rocky outcrops and ruined Mogul forts, mosques and palaces, this was quite different country. The vegetation rose rich and strong, coloured in many shades of vivid green. Here, the problem is one of too much water rather than too little

of it. Dykes, canals and ditches were brimming; the fields
sodden and soggy. In lagoons on either side of the rough
road naked brown children splashed among the pale mauve
water hyacinths.

At the station there was no Darrel, for he had arrived
early and gone to look for us, but at length the three of us
were assembled in the waiting-room and heard his story.
The Customs officials at Calcutta had given him a rough
going over, for to reach Gauhati by rail he had to pass
through Eastern Pakistan. Fear was expressed that he
might be just another person trying to smuggle goods
through to the Moslems. The collapsible boats and the tents
were at first condemned as military stores. Then the locks
on some of Frank's cases had to be broken in order that the
contents might be examined. There had been a fierce argument over two bottles of brandy and a bottle of rum which
was to be our iron liquor ration. Finally matters had been
smoothed over by a discreet conversation in a dark corner
of the station. This explained an obscure item of £6 on
Darrel's expense account.

We were still a day and a half's journey by rail from Lokra
and we decided that Darrel had better come with us in case
some last minute requests should arise from our meeting
with Stonor. With Darrel's stores and our own baggage
we now had twenty-five pieces in all. These required an
army of porters and three taxis to shift.

From Gauhati it was necessary to cross the Brahmaputra
by ferry to catch our next connection. The crossing was
chiefly notable for our first clear view of a Brahamputra
Blind Dolphin, lazily dipping and rolling in our bow wave.
This we felt was a little lesson in zoology which might come
in useful. The sky was pale mauve, purple and gold above
the green water; rain was in the air and a storm duly broke.

That evening saw us in Rangiya, an out-of-the-way
junction whence we were to catch the night train to Lokra.
All that we saw of Rangiya in the dusk of the evening was

a line of tiny thatched bazaar shops, shaded by coconut palms and lining a single dusty road. The bazaar was murmurous with the hum of low pitched voices, and smelled sweetly of richly spiced foods cooking in flat brass pans over glowing charcoal fires.

Back at the station a pleasant surprise awaited us. The refreshment room was in charge of a tall, grey-haired Indian who had spent many years as cook to a European officers mess. So we dined well that evening of chicken soup, curried chicken, roast chicken and crème caramel. This we topped off with half a bottle of Indian gin.

Thudding and clanking along the narrow-gauge Lokra line between walls of close-pressing jungle we had a jolting, uncomfortable night. Cramped beside our mountain of luggage in the only first-class compartment, we were continuously pestered by mosquitoes, and on one occasion by a trapped hornet.

At six the next morning we arrived at the terminus, weary and travel-grimed, to find no Stonor. This might have proved a serious matter. In a moment of panic we imagined that the porters must have deserted; or possibly Stonor, tired of waiting, had pushed on alone. The explanation was, however, the obvious one. Half an hour later Stonor arrived. He had not received the express cable announcing our late arrival, which we had sent him eighteen hours before from Gauhati; he had turned up at the station on the off-chance that we might be on the train. There was no porter trouble; many of the Dafla porters had themselves not yet arrived.

CHAPTER VI

# Lokra

WE WERE DRINKING TINY CUPS OF STICKY TEA AT A STATION
stall when Stonor drove up. With him, we now walked
back to the train while Frank set up his film camera. I
re-entered the first-class compartment and stepped out of
it for the formal introduction: "Charles Stonor—Ralph
Izzard." We repeated this manœuvre three times while
Stonor wondered what on earth he had been let in for, and a
bewildered posse of porters raised and lowered luggage in
unison. Frank, however, was adamant. He needed a defini-
tive shot for the opening of the Buru film, and he could
think of nothing better than a hand-shaking "Charles Stonor,
I presume!" sequence in front of the signboard "Rangapara
(North)", which was the railway station for Lokra. If the
ceremony achieved nothing else, it did at least put us all on
Christian name terms.

Charles had brought with him a 15 cwt. truck and into
this we piled our luggage and ourselves. A speedy journey
of ten miles now brought us to a tremendous breakfast and
hot baths in the Political Officer's bungalow at Charduar, a
short distance down the road from Lokra. This bungalow
was a spacious, comfortable home of two stories, built
of timber and white plaster and surrounded by wide
verandas. It stood in two acres of well-kept lawn
decorated with flower-beds of roses, dahlias and hibiscus.
The whole was enclosed by a neat, waist-high hedge beyond
which stretched park-land in which stood stately trees of
many varieties. The park ended abruptly at the edge of the
jungle, above whose frayed and tattered outline could be
seen the faint blue silhouettes of the Balipara Hills.

About the garden flew scarlet-seated paroquets, their wing and dorsal feathers the vivid green colour of a new leaf. The air smelled damp and fresh, and we wandered about our new home in a happy state of excitement and invigoration.

When we arrived Robert Menzies, the Political Officer, was away on tour, but he had left us a note urging us to make ourselves thoroughly comfortable.

That morning we had a final sorting out of gear on the veranda and distributed the loads, as far as possible, into forty-pound units. After pruning away non-essentials we were still left with a formidable mountain of luggage, but I was later to appreciate with what care and forethought Charles had selected our exact requirements. Nothing went with us which we did not make full use of, except the two collapsible boats; finally it became a question of having too little supplies rather than too much. We allowed ourselves only forty pounds each of personal kit, clothes, boots, books, writing materials and so on. We made one brief store purchasing excursion down to the lines of the 5th Assam Rifles, where we met Lt.-Col. Frank Noble, the commanding officer, who genially exposed wrists and ankles to display dim-dam and leech bites, the scars, he said, of a recent trip into the jungle. These would be in store for us in plenty, but one soon got used to them.

Back at the bungalow we were introduced to the servants who would be coming with us on the expedition. In order of their appearance they were the following:

Orenimo, the bearer, of the head-hunting tribe of Lhota Nagas.* Orenimo was now westernised and wore bush-shirt, shorts and boots, but he still cherished a photograph of himself in full tribal regalia. He was a handsome, capable

* Writing of the Lhota Nagas in "The Golden Bough", Sir James Fraser says: "Once they flayed a boy alive, carved him in pieces, and distributed the flesh among all the villagers, who put it into their corn-bins to avert bad luck and ensure plentiful crops of grain." I am assured that local investigation has failed to produce any evidence whatsoever in support of this particular story, but the Lhota Nagas have, of course, remained head-hunters up to very recent times.

good-tempered fellow, ever smiling. Like all people of primitive origin, he was given to laughing uproariously at the misfortunes of others, and it was some time before he could control himself after first viewing the complicated system of strappings and bandages in which I remained encased for some weeks. Nevertheless, until I was again capable of dressing and bathing myself, I found him as tender with me as a mother. He was particularly fond of bathing people, and while he massaged my back, he would "Shush-shush" away through his teeth as if he were grooming a horse.

He came from a clan who prefer singing to dancing; he had a good tenor voice, had picked up many western songs and hymns, and would croon away to himself for hours on end.

Orenimo had a secret which was never mentioned in front of him. He had an aunt who was a witch, renowned for some remarkable cures of tribal maladies, and whose "familiar" was a snake in the jungle. As Frank said: "The only way to embarrass Orenimo is to ask: 'How's that old witch of an aunt of yours?' " A test, which, of course, we never made.

Pio Pio: assistant to Orenimo and a distant Naga relative of his. Pio Pio was a bright intelligent lad of about sixteen. He was a good-looking boy, devoted to Orenimo, but with none of his cousin's sophistication and worldliness.

Washington the cook: a Christian convert from the Kasi tribe wherein the women entirely dominate the men. Washington was a good cook and had he been able to knit he would probably have made an ideal husband for a Kasi wife. By escaping to Christianity—he was an American Baptist convert, hence his astonishing name—he had not escaped matrimony. He was reputed to have a huge family, and on that account no doubt relished the prospect of two or three months away from home in the jungle. He looked a typical hen-pecked little man, middle-aged, with tired drooping moustache and poor physique, but somehow, on the march, he was always among the first in camp, still fresh enough to cope efficiently and immediately with what were at times atrocious cooking conditions.

Tameng, an orphan of the Apa Tani tribe, destitute and down on his luck in Lokra. How this graceful youth with flowing raven hair came to attach himself to the party none seemed to know, but he proved a godsend. He was tireless as a weaver and rough carpenter about camp and he was the equal of any Dafla in jungle-craft, in fact we came to look upon him as a tame Tarzan.

Taning and Padme, two Dafla interpreters. These two youths had been living in Lokra for some years, and had picked up western dress and habits as well as Assamese dialect. Taning, the senior, was a bouncing, boisterous young man, for ever chattering, always very full of himself. He was inclined to look down upon the hill Daflas as "savages", to treat them with tolerant amusement, and thus he frequently put them out of countenance during an important interrogation. We suffered him for his never-failing good spirits; Taning enjoyed every minute of the trip, and was eager that everyone should know it. Also he was unquestionably loyal.

Apart from the servants, the other object of note was Charles's shaggy, ginger-coloured, mongrel sheep-dog who rejoiced in the name of "Kiro", which in Naga dialect means "The Open Flower". This name was one of Orenimo's brainwaves. The only flower one could possibly liken the dog to, was a wind-blown chrysanthemum.

That afternoon the Dafla porters began to collect under a huge pine tree beyond the garden hedge.

Some were Lokra Dafla settlers wearing odd items of European dress, but the majority were braves from the hills, with Mongoloid features, well built with strongly developed thighs and calves. Messengers had drummed them out of the mountains on the promise of a rich reward for a few days' work as porters, and because their late harvest had been a poor one, they were glad enough to come. They were to receive one silver rupee plus four pounds of rice and a quantity of salt per day. Wearing feathered head-dresses, carrying bows and arrows and gathered in their present setting they formed a picture which would have served wonderfully well as an illustration for a book by Fenimore Cooper.

A warrior, taken at random, can be described as follows: Most conspicuous is the head-dress. This consists of a woven cane skull-cap surmounted by a crest of a hornbill beak, dyed scarlet, tip to the rear. Beneath the tip of the beak, and jutting out over the neck, lies a black and white barred hornbill feather. The hair is screwed in a bun over the forehead, transfixed by a foot-long horizontal skewer which holds the skull-cap in place. A band of cane, threaded with metal studs, is bound round the head beneath the cap. The lobes of the ears are pierced and stretched and contain ornaments the width of napkin rings. Round the throat is hung a collection of yellow, blue and green necklaces, prized as heirlooms, and as such having a reputed local value of about £20 each, though the same necklace can be bought from a Tibetan trader in Delhi for a few shillings.

The main garment is a length of cloth woven from pulped nettles, shapeless, knotted over each shoulder and reaching half-way down the thighs. The chest is protected by a broad band of bison skin and the lower body by many coils of plaited cane. Garters of blue thread are wound tightly round the legs between calf and knee.

Armament consists of two daos, or swords, in bamboo sheaths hung round the neck on thongs of hide. The frogs of the sheaths are ornamented by bears' teeth or boars' tushes.

Of the daos, the smaller is a general utility instrument, while the larger, sometimes about two and a half feet long serves as weapon or felling axe, but is most often unsheathed for slashing a path through the jungle. Many Daflas carry five-foot-long bamboo bows and cane quivers full of arrows. A poison paste, made from pulped aconite plants, is kneaded round the shaft immediately below the metal heads of the arrows used for big game hunting. This poison can allegedly kill a wounded bear in twenty minutes. A coil of plaited human hair is wound round the left wrist as protection against an awkwardly released bow string.

All wear a pouch made of hide or monkey skin slung over the shoulder, and all when travelling carry a knapsack of woven cane.

Priests are dressed as others and carry the same weapons, but down their backs they hang an eagles'-wing fan as emblem of office.

Headmen, invested with a degree of authority by Government, wear a presentation scarlet tunic.

The women wear their hair in plaits wound round the head. Their necklaces are more numerous and their nettle cloth garments reach half-way down the calf. Instead of the knee garter, they wear ankle bands twisted so tightly as to deform their legs and cause them much pain. They chew betel nut incessantly which stains their teeth dark red and, like the men, are seldom seen without a foul-smelling pipe between their lips.

These then, were the people among whom we were to live during the next few weeks and who were to be our companions in the hunt for the buru.

After dinner that evening, while the three of us were seated in Menzies' sitting-room, Charles explained to us something of the country into which we were going. The broad band of jungle-covered mountains stretching from the Brahmaputra to the Thibetan frontier was exceedingly little explored. The area we were to penetrate was only very roughly surveyed and he was the only European, to his knowledge, who had ever visited the Rilo swamp where the buru was supposed to exist. Up there it was no use measuring distances in miles. It might be a month of stiff marching from Lokra to Thibet, but no European had ever completed the journey. Parts of the country were very malarial and previous parties, unequipped with modern drugs, had invariably been forced to turn back after losing porters.

We would normally have a trek of about ten days ahead of us, but at this time of year it would be possible to cover the first twenty-five miles into the foothills by truck. Our plan was to reach Rilo before the rains came. If we were lucky with the weather, it was just possible that there would come a time when enough rain had fallen to enable the buru to appear, yet not enough to make our journey back to Lokra impossible. In such case we might make a dash for it, at the cost of jettisoning equipment. It was more probable, how-ever, that we should be marooned in Rilo throughout the rains. This explained why we should have to carry food with us for at least three months, for we could rely on obtaining little or nothing to eat from the countryside itself. And that was why, in its turn, we had had to engage a seemingly endless chain of porters: porters to carry our own gear and food; porters to carry the rice and salt for their own pay and food; porters to carry the gear of the porters who carried the food, and so on. In all, and counting Sir Akbar's Gurkhas, we mustered 120 men. In other words, forty men were needed in order to put one European into a position whence he could view the buru. This was obvi-ously one of the main arguments why the area had never been properly explored and why the buru, up till then, had not been discovered.

The Daflas, Charles said, were spread right across the Balipara Frontier Tract, into which we were going, and in fact occupied several thousand square miles of the Outer Himalayas, living at altitudes varying from 500 to 8,000 feet. Their strength has never been estimated, but is likely to be at least two hundred thousand.

5

Their relationships have not yet been investigated, but they almost certainly belong to the so-called Tibeto-Burman stock, and are related to the Kachins, Mishmis and other tribes of the India-Burma-China border region. Their original home was very possibly in the North Burma, Eastern China area. They have certainly been in their present home many centuries.

External trade is largely confined to salt, which is unknown in the Balipara hills; thus the Daflas are forced to make frequent journeys to the plains in search of it. It is by regulating the supply of salt, that a judicious political officer can obtain docile obedience over vast areas which he otherwise would never hope to administer single-handed. The Daflas obtain some bell metal from Thibet which they fashion into tobacco pipes by means of the "cire perdue" method. Until recent years, the Daflas often raided tea-gardens near the southern foothills, carrying off coolie women for slaves, but they are now kept under reasonable control. Daflas to the north of Rilo were known to be truculent and did not allow travellers to pass through their territory.

At Rilo and surrounding villages an epidemic of chicken-pox had broken out, and as this had appeared for the first time it was proving particularly virulent, and had killed off about thirty people. We should therefore have to be careful to do nothing to offend the Spirits, for should any unorthodox behaviour of ours coincide with further deaths, things might become awkward. At the same time one could bear in mind that a common trick of all the frontier tribes was to spread news of an epidemic ahead of a European party in the hope of diverting it from their villages. It was their experience that Europeans were inclined to ask too many embarrassing questions!

Our talk then switched to a discussion of the buru itself. Tales of strange animals which exist, or may have existed, in the remote vastnesses of Assam are, of course, common enough. For instance, there is a belief, founded on fairly sound biological reasoning, that somewhere, some day, a black tiger will fall to a hunter's rifle. Black panther are comparatively plentiful in certain parts of Assam. The blackness of the coat is accounted for by excessive pigmentation in the skin. A black panther is, in fact, the opposite of an albino panther. Albino tiger have been recorded; but never to my knowledge has anyone ever shot or seen a black tiger. Yet why not? Then there is the tale of two tea-planters on shikar at the edge of a vast swamp near Sadiya. As the sun set one evening both men were startled to hear the sounds of a huge ponderous animal wallowing in the swamp. As they approached they were amazed to see a reptilian head raise itself on an endless neck above the reeds. Both men fired, but apparently without effect, for the animal turned and heaved its vast bulk away to the centre of the swamp whither it could not be followed.

Then that very morning Frank Noble had told us that a tradition existed among his men of the Assam Rifles, for the most part recruited from Gurkha settlers, that in the none too distant past a gigantic animal had been seen to cross the Brahmaputra and take refuge in the mountains to the north, where it was still supposed to survive.

So much for freaks and fantasies. We, on our part, resolutely refused to classify the buru with either. We ran through all the animals which could possibly fit the description given to us by the Apa Tanis and the Daflas and drew blank. Our final verdict at that time was, "probably a hitherto unknown animal; just possibly a prehistoric one".

Of the existence of *something* we had no doubt. To others outside our immediate circle who had been told of the object of our mission, we had cautiously pointed out that they must reckon with more than fifty per cent chance of total failure, and had advised against pre-publicity. Among ourselves, that night, we optimistically rated the chances of success at about seventy per cent. Thus we talked far into the night: Charles, the eager, earnest zoologist, with a monopoly of knowledge of local conditions. Frank, the ex-Indian Army officer at home in any jungle; myself the unknown quantity, temporarily crippled, a jungle tiro and with nothing to offer except a wartime sailor's knowledge of practical seamanship, bends and hitches, small boat management and the like. My knowledge might come in useful, again it might not.

# CHAPTER VII

# Lokra—Seidjhosa

THE NEXT DAY BROKE FINE AND CLEAR AND LITTLE TIME was lost in loading stores into the vehicles. By 9 a.m. the convoy was ready to move off. It consisted of one 15 cwt. truck with myself in the place of honour beside the driver, as this promised the most comfortable going; then Frank and Charles in the jeep and trailer; finally two truck-loads of Daflas.

As we moved out from beneath the cool porch Frank was poised on the lawn to record "the departure from civilisation". Passing through the lines of the Assam Rifles, we found Noble waiting by the wayside to wish us "God speed". Beyond, the road curved through immaculate tea gardens, the trim leaves gleaming as if they had been dipped in green lacquer. Half an hour's bumpy going—which had me hugging my arm to take the shock out of the jolting— brought us to the banks of the Bharelly where a crude ferry consisting of two pontoons propelled by an outboard motor, soon landed the lot of us on the far side. Thence, the road pointed to hills, tea gardens giving place to patches of jungle, until, after twenty-five miles the jungle opened out on a vast meadow of elephant grass which reached to the banks of the Pakke River, an off-shoot of the Bharelly. This spot, known as Seidjhosa, is a regular Dafla camping-ground. The grass had been cut back and two rotting huts served the Daflas as rest-houses. Before us the Pakke ran smoothly and noiselessly over a bed of rounded boulders. On the far side began the jungle proper, spreading, in an unbroken carpet, up to and over the first range of 2,000 feet high hills. It was here, in previous years, Charles had seen herds of wild elephant drinking, a black panther playing with two cubs, and that rare bird the Great Heron which reputedly stands five feet high.

In camp the Daflas proved a feckless lot, contenting them-selves with erecting rough lean-tos of bamboo and wild banana fronds for their own occupation. They then began weaving baskets in which to carry their loads. That finished, they started agitating for higher wages, a move which Charles firmly and speedily crushed.

In contrast, the Gurkha porters set to with a will. Cutting and hacking with their kukris they soon erected two sizeable huts, a table and three chairs, a bath-room and a latrine, all of which would have served us for weeks. With them worked the Apa Tani, Tameng, screwing his flowing locks into a bun at the nape of his neck and chip-chopping away tire-lessly with his dao.

Hardly had our three diminutive tents been set up when a deafening monsoon thunderstorm broke, accompanied by what amounted to a cloud-burst and each of us dived for his tent to ride out the storm. Frank, who had been given the largest tent by reason of his bulkier equipment, was soon flooded out. Charles and I, in our tiny one-man Everest models with sewn in ground-sheets remained dry, but there were times when the side of my tent strained and bellied out like a sail in a gale and I began to fear, seriously, that the entire tent would be bodily uprooted, pegs and all, and blown with me in it into the Pakke. Had this happened I should never have got out of the normal exit with my arm strapped to my side, and I half thought of unsheathing my knife in readiness to cut my way through the side when the crisis came.

With the passing of the storm, three planters, who had been fishing, arrived on an elephant. One of these, M., was well-known to Charles as a mighty hunter with more tigers to his credit than any other man in Assam. He was also tough in other respects. The story goes that on one

occasion, in the first-floor bar of the Shillong Club, he
laughed so heartily at a joke that he fell backwards out of a
window.    Horrified, the rest of the party rushed from the
room expecting to find M. dead.  Instead, they met him half-
way down the stairs, trotting upward as if nothing unusual
had occurred.  He had turned a complete somersault and
landed safely on his feet.

All three were immensely curious as to why we should be
heading for the hills at the start of the rainy season, which
they considered madness.  Charles, with complete composure, told a long story of a proposed investigation of
irrigation conditions.  We had no desire to disclose our
secret.  We were determined to be first in the field.  Also we
felt under a moral obligation not to encourage trophy
hunters, at least until proper measures had been taken to
protect the buru.

At tea there was a minor incident when a scorpion fell
out of a tree above us on to the middle of our table.  It was
promptly dispatched by Charles.

That evening Frank set out along the river bank with a
light Mauser rifle in the hope of bagging a barking deer as it
came down to drink.  Night fell, however, before any game
stirred.

Our possession of a rifle had won us much prestige
among the Daflas; our failure to provide them with any
fresh meat as encouragement was also noted.

After supper we had scarcely time to get back to the
inevitable subject of the buru before another storm broke.
Each of us again made for his tent, and as the storm showed
no sign of abating we turned in, while white lightning lit
the wild dark countryside about as vividly as by magnesium
flare.

# CHAPTER VIII

# Seidjhosa—Takko Senyak

BY FIVE A.M. THE NEXT MORNING THE WEATHER HAD AGAIN cleared leaving only a few woolly clouds sliding low across the face of the higher ranges. With an easy stage of only six miles in front of us there was no trouble in getting the porters started, and soon the long line of 120 men was stretched out in single file through the elephant grass. The trail at first doubled back to the jungle and then turned left upstream and parallel to the river.

The track was broad, though much overgrown, and resembled an avenue in any neglected European forest. Among the fresh green grass there was even a sheen as of blue-bells, for here a pale blue flowering weed, whose leaves are pulped and used for stemming the bleeding from leech bites, grew in profusion. The vegetation soon grew denser, however, masses of vines and creepers climbing avidly up the trunks and branches of the trees until they had all the appearance of hanging gardens with clusters of golden brown orchids nodding down at us from the summits.

After two miles we again came out on the banks of the Pakke. A cliff, deeply bitten into by past floods rose steeply to our right, and it became necessary to ford the stream. At this time of year the water was running swiftly and about two feet deep, so that the current tugged strongly at the legs as one floundered over the smooth, slippery stones of the bed. This was difficult going for me, and even the Gurkhas and Daflas were forced to hold hands to keep balance beneath their loads. It was questionable whether the river was likely to be still fordable after a further two months of rain, or could even then be crossed in our rubber boats.

On the far side some of the Daflas were already resting, and it became apparent that we had two sets to deal with: first, the hill people who had come down from their homes specially for the occasion. These were still unspoilt, anxious to do a good job of work, earn their pay and then scatter to their villages. Homeward bound they were no trouble. Secondly, the Lokra Daflas, many of them renegade outcasts from the hill villages. The majority of these had been spoilt by contacts in the plains, they were experts at dodging the heavier loads, they had no intention of moving fast outward bound, and they were at the bottom of the pay troubles. Of all the Daflas it was true that they preferred the steep ascents and descents of the hills to the level slog over the boulders beside the river bed which now faced us. Only the Gurkha party plugged on steadily and silently.

From the river, which we were forced to recross after two miles, we finally turned into dense swamp jungle where the vegetation grows so swiftly during the rains that the path has to be cut afresh every few days. A sudden, steep climb brought us to a small clearing where stands the Dafla village of Lenko. This village consists of two long, low thatched houses built on stilts, each containing conceivably as many as a hundred people.

On an open platform at the end of one of the houses stood the village priest wearing the Government's scarlet cloak of authority. The priest proved an enlightened and cordial man who invited us up to his platform, and cheerfully posed for a photograph in front of his sacrificial posts and tablets which were crudely scrawled with poker work designs and hung with the skulls and bones of slaughtered animals.

A further mile through swampy vegetation brought us to the second camp site, a small green platform of turf in a narrow ravine down which tumbled, from pool to pool, a stream of pure, sparkling water. On either bank a dark green curtain of jungle vines and creepers rose almost vertically for hundreds of feet. Bamboo was plentiful, however, and soon the forest resounded once more to dao and kukri, and in an incredibly short space of time a camp as comfortable and complete as that of the night before stood waiting for us.

That evening Charles, who never missed an opportunity to interrogate a Dafla about the buru, came to us and trying to suppress his obvious excitement, informed us that he had just learned that the Rilo swamp was already filled with water, and that the buru had already been seen this year!

"I give you the information for what it is worth," he added.

In spite of the caution which we all tried to preserve at all times, we could not help feeling that the information was worth quite a lot. There had been an unusually heavy rainfall during March, therefore, it was by no means improbable that the swamp had, indeed, filled early and consequently it was possible that the buru had already made his bow.

Now that we had surmounted the major obstacles of launching the expedition; now that we had crossed beyond the frontier of civilisation, and were perched in virtually unexplored country only a few days' march from Rilo swamp, the final tracking down of the buru had begun to look suspiciously like a picnic. We, the chosen three, destined to give the buru to the scientific world, were elated. To the question: "What is the buru?" we now added: "What shall we do when we get it?" Would we be justified in shooting a single specimen, or should we content ourselves with trying to lasso it with the coils of rope we had brought with us, photograph it, and then turn it loose again? One thing we were agreed upon. There would be little sense in taking one quick look at the buru and then rushing back with the story. To do so would be to invite a stream of trophy hunters who would still be able to get up to Rilo and back before the rains set in for good. We should not only lose our full year's advantage over rival expeditions; the whole buru population would stand a good chance of being wiped out before proper measures could be taken to declare the area a game preserve. In the end we decided that, if it was to be as easy as it looked, we should in any case be well advised to spend at least six weeks getting as complete a record as possible, both of the appearance and habits of the buru, in order that we might present it as a solid scientific fact, leaving no room for doubt about the desirability of its immediate protection.

With the buru in the bag and our reputations made, we played with future plans. Jokingly we planned to take out a patent for a buru children's toy, to be launched on the market next Christmas. The black tiger once more came up for review as our next objective. Frank and I discussed the possibility of searching the Sadiya swamp for the planters' "monster". Charles refused to follow us here; he felt that the discovery of one live dinosaur was as much as any zoologist had a right to expect!

That night we turned in with high hopes and slept well.

The next morning there was a far more earnest air about the camp. While we were finishing breakfast the hill Daflas were already squatting down, easing themselves into the bark headbands of their carrying baskets, helping each other to their feet and moving off. The Lokra Daflas remained behind to squabble over the distribution of the lighter kitchen loads. It was obviously to be a hard day.

The trail began by rising sheer up the far wall of the ravine; thence it wound its way through clumps of flowering and dying bamboo to the summit of the first ridge. I tackled this stretch light-heartedly in the belief that the top of the first ridge would bring easier going, but far from it! It proved merely the first and lowest of a dozen such ridges, each mounting ever higher, with the topmost ones still wreathed in clouds. In figures, we were to climb that day from 500 to 6,000 feet, and what with altitude lost owing to intermittent descents, we must have climbed half as much again. To add to my difficulties—mine especially, as less than a week before I had been only able to walk haltingly a few hundred yards—the path was slippery and treacherous beyond belief. Its coating of damp leaves and moss hid loose rocks, roots and creepers; obstacles which reoccurred in never ending variation, every few yards. At times the path rose so steeply that every foot had to be fought for, and progress literally became a matter for all fours. It was not long before I could make only a few hundred yards at a time without sinking down to rest on some log or boulder. All this time, and for the rest of the day, the way led through dank, lifeless jungle. Trees with wide-splayed roots rose over a hundred feet above us, their branches festooned with creepers and vines. The undergrowth was a series of dark green curtains relieved only occasionally by pale green, quivering bamboo thickets. Anything less like the romantic conception of jungle—tribes of chattering monkeys, clouds of shrieking, gaudy paroquets, snakes dropping off trees— could scarcely be imagined. Seen at its worst, or near worst, this jungle was damp, dismal, depressing, much like an abandoned shrubbery in an English autumn. Only an occasional fallen flower gave any hint of glorious orchids flourishing beyond the green ceiling above our heads.

Feeling as wretched as I have ever felt I plodded on, Charles keeping beside me. He, with calves of steel and a reputation as a demon pace-maker even among the Daflas, could have made light of the going, but very graciously he stayed by me never giving a hint of impatience.

It was not long before we came on the first discarded loads; those naturally of the Lokra Daflas. They had been dumped by the wayside by porters who had given up the struggle, and sloped off into the bushes to await our passing before turning back for home. We had expected something of the sort and had engaged twenty extra porters for just such an emergency. We thus made light of the matter. Some time after we discovered that a number of the kerosene tins had been punctured in what must have been a last frenzied search for rum. Later inspection also showed that a number of other stores had been pilfered. A personal loss was six cakes of toilet soap and two tins of talcum powder from the pockets of my rucksack. For what purpose the Daflas required the soap, unless for eating, I do not know; it was certainly never used for washing.

There had been no sign of wild life in the jungle except the occasional eerie shriek of a bird rising in fright at our approach, but half-way through the morning I came on a small snake. It was about two feet long, nut brown, with yellow and orange markings, of a species which Charles had never seen before. Obligingly it slid off the path, coiled itself in a bush and cocked its head and about three inches of its length. That was all it ever did do, for a passing Dafla whipped out his dao and sliced it neatly into three eight-inch segments.

All this time, Charles and I had been carrying on a conversation, or rather Charles had been carrying on a running commentary interspersed with grunts by myself.

First Charles pointed out a clump of bamboo, now fully grown and dying, and in flower for the first and only time at the end of its ten-year life. The seeds dropping from the flowers have an irresistible attraction for rats and other jungle rodents. After feasting on the seeds, the rats increase enormously in number and having picked the jungle floor clean beneath the bamboo they turn to the peasants' crops. In the past some of these depredations have been so severe that whole villages of Daflas have been forced to migrate to avoid starvation. This was the sort of problem in tribal agriculture that Charles was supposed to deal with; but he had found no logical explanation for this rodent phenomenon, except possibly that the bamboo seed acted as an aphrodisiac on the rat, leading to vastly increased reproduction.

Most of our conversation, however, centred round the buru, a subject none of us ever tired of. After an hour or so's silence Charles would suddenly come out with some such remark as: "There *must* be a snag, but I just *cannot* see it!" And we would be at it again. Along that endless march as I plodded painfully upwards, Charles developed a new theory that the buru might be a gigantic newt or salamander. This, he felt, would be almost as interesting as a dinosaur, for a newt as big as an ox would be no less remarkable than a frog the size of a cart-horse!

Towards noon we began to pass groups of resting Daflas, later on in turn to be passed by them. Once or twice we came on Frank's great red face waiting in ambush for us with his camera. Stripped to the waist he, too, was finding the going hard, particularly as he had to be dodging back and forth continually with his equipment.

The time came when, almost weeping with vexation and helplessness, I sank down on a log incapable for the moment of going farther, yet knowing I could not remain where I was. It was then that a brave named Kolu, seeing my plight, slipped his load and came to the rescue. Making a quick cast round the jungle he selected a tree and, shinning up it, was soon hacking and thrashing among the branches. Down fluttered a leafy bough carrying fruits as big as golf-balls. These were known to the Daflas as "kongna". They had a light brown husk and a fleshy interior like a lychee, but they were as bitter as can be conceived. As an astringent thirst quencher they suited the occasion admirably; on any western dessert table they would be an abomination.

Another hour's stumbling progress brought me to a small dell cupped in the mountainside, and here a Dafla woman produced a brass bowl of ice-cold water, drawn none knew whence. This I drained gratefully, and although it should have given me dysentery, it did not.

Finally, tottering on wobbling legs, I was on the point of giving in, when once more we caught the welcome and none too distant sound of dao and kukri "thock, thocking", against bamboo. A moment later we heard Kiro, the dog,

bark. The next camp was thus within earshot, but nevertheless it was a full half hour before I could summon enough
energy to cover the remaining four hundred odd yards. The
day's march, which had given me the most strenuous exercise
of my life was over, and I collapsed full length and utterly
spent, on a bundle of rolled tarpaulins.

# CHAPTER IX

# Takko Senyak—Rilo

THAT AFTERNOON WASHINGTON THE UNSMILING, READER of the unspoken thought, provided tea sharply laced with native spirit. I topped this off with a bamboo stoop of rice beer, but it was some time before I could find any appetite for food.

Takko Senyak, or "the jungle camp", was on the crest of a range 6,000 feet high. The site was merely a clearing in the jungle, a halt for a single night, with no water to wash away the sweat of the day. But we were too tired to worry about washing, and after an early supper we rolled wearily into bed and slept like the dead.

The next day we all felt much restored. We were promised an easier march—an initial climb of 1,000 feet, then a long gradual descent to the upper reaches of the Pakke River.

The whole camp was in good spirits.

We had scarcely moved off from the camp when the jungle appeared to thin somewhat, and before long we came out on a knife-edge ridge with the sides falling almost sheer for hundreds of feet on either hand. To the north, purple, mauve and violet ranges stretched in endless succession to the snows. To the south, the way we had come, there was, however, already a comfortable number of ridges separating us from the now invisible Brahmaputra Plain. All around us, at lower altitude, the jungle spread unbroken over mountain and valley like a gigantic crumpled green eiderdown.

Another bout of stiff climbing brought us at length to the 7,000-foot mark, and with it the highest point of the entire march. Here, by the path, stood an immense moss-grown boulder. On passing it each Dafla plucked a spray of green

leaves from a bush, slapped his ankle with it, and then cast
the spray on a rapidly growing pile atop the boulder. This
simple rite of sympathetic magic represented that the peak
exertion had been reached; past tiredness was therefore
bidden to depart from the leg to the twig as soon as it
touched the ankle. The rest of the day was a long unevent-
ful amble down easy gradients until suddenly the green
curtain of jungle lifted, and we came out on the slopes
immediately overhanging the upper Pakke Valley. Here a
rough attempt had been made to clear the jungle by crudely
hacking down trees with daos and then burning them.
Between the ensuing tangle of charred and rotting trunks
and boughs patches of rice and millet had been planted. This
wasteful and expensive system is all the Dafla manages to
achieve in the way of desultory agriculture. As soon as one
crop has been harvested the cleared area, or "jhoom", is
abandoned, it being more troublesome to tackle the next
year's weeds and secondary vegetation than to fell a fresh
area of primary jungle.

While resting on the "jhoom" we made out the two or
three long low houses, far below in the valley, which com-
prise Pakke Village. Beyond, rose another steep and forbidding range, to be climbed on the next day's march.

The Pakke River site, where we were to spend the night,
looked ideal for every purpose. Where we reached the bank,
the stream made an almost complete curve, leaving what
amounted to an island, some two hundred yard across, in
mid-stream. It was on this island, after fording the river,
that we set up camp. Around us rose dense jungle in a
magnificent circular sweep enclosing the site like the tiers
of a vast green amphitheatre. There was water in plenty for
everyone here and promise of good fishing. In addition, an
abundance of tattered wild banana fronds and bamboo stems
for the Dafla lean-tos. There was also a multitude of dim-
dam flies which raise a maddeningly irritating blood-blister
before one realises one is bitten. This I found out speedily

6

when I stripped to wash, and in less time than it takes to say I was back, unwashed, in my clothes again. Dim-dams are most active in bright sunlight and normally one enjoys relief when the shadows lengthen. But at Pakke, at sundown, the mosquitoes took charge.

The next morning showed that one of the Gurkhas had gone down with malaria. Him we left, uncomplaining, with one of his companions, to be picked up by the returning party of temporary porters when they came back that way a few days later.

The only thing I care to remember about the Pakke camp was a handsome orchid which Charles discovered growing immediately above our dinner table. This we plucked while in bud, for transfer to the Rilo camp.

This last day of the trek was to be a stiff one; no one made any secret of that fact, but all of us were buoyed up by the thought that there would be rest unlimited at the end of it. I had begun to realise, too, that I was growing stronger, not weaker, as the days passed; I was finding my mountain legs. Nevertheless, the first 4,000-foot climb was a severe one. Charles had pushed on ahead to select a good camp site at Rilo, leaving Frank and I to come on at our leisure. Frank was anxious to shoot some more film and was in no hurry. This was just as well, for there had been another heavy fall of rain in the night, and the path was greasier and more difficult than anything we had yet experienced. For this section I had plenty of strength, but was unable to keep my feet. Finally, with Orenimo pegging each foot as I kicked a fresh toe-hold, and grinning hugely at my antics, I made some sort of scrambling progress. There were one or two hectic moments. First I slipped beyond recovery, and came down heavily on my injured shoulder. In falling I had let out a yell of anticipatory pain, but in actual fact I hardly felt the blow at all; a first sign that the bone was knit and the injury healed. Then gyrating madly on one foot and waving my stick in my free hand I nearly fell flat on my face on top of a snake of the same species we had seen before. A moment's inspection showed that it was stone dead, its back broken by someone just ahead of us.

We then discovered that the rain had brought out the first leeches. Frank claimed six in various stages of satiety on each calf; I, in an old pair of sea boots, escaped.

Noon saw us over the last range and two hours later, after a gradual descent, we came out on the rim of Rilo Valley. Here our hopes rose at once, for as a possible dwelling place for "extinct" animals, it was almost as feasible a location as the plateau of Conan Doyle's *Lost World*.

The valley forms an almost perfect basin, about three square miles in extent. The floor is about four thousand feet above sea level, while the rim of mountains which enclose it, towers upwards for another two thousand feet. The rim, roughly circular, is broken only by one narrow rocky gorge, which would be impassable for any animal of the type we were seeking. Dramatically then, the setting was all we had expected.

The path along the top of the ridge had been faint enough, but the fork down which we turned for the valley was scarcely discernible except for the improvements made by our own party. Travelling through the jungle the Dafla invariably carries his dao unsheathed and cuts and slashes at overhanging boughs, or notches footholds in fallen trees, as he passes. He does this more to relieve the monotony of the march than in any spirit of helpfulness towards his fellow men, but the effect is to keep the jungle paths in what may be described as a state of good repair. This is certainly true of the passage of a large party such as ours was. However, there was not much one could do to improve the path to Rilo. It dropped sheer through the trees down what amounted to a precipice. This would have defeated me entirely had not the patient Frank climbed down ahead of me, and placed each of my feet in position before I ventured a fresh step. As it was, I fell twice, jarred myself badly and shook my new-found confidence in my collar-bone. This painful descent of many hundred feet brought us at last to a gentler slope down which rushed a torrent of clear water over a firm gravel bottom. About us the vegetation had taken on all the aspect of a primeval forest. Giant ferns, vines and creepers swathed the taller trees, while between them grew an impenetrable thicket of cane, bamboo, taloned screw-pine and other fleshy plants. Through this barrier the stream had carved itself a tunnel, and down this we splashed for a further twenty minutes. Finally, the path, by now only inches wide, turned off into the cane thicket. At length the green twilight which enclosed us lightened, and we emerged into a clearing in the jungle about 300 yards across and roughly circular. This clearing was part of a shelf formed from silt brought down by the mountain streams. It had been recently cultivated but was now left derelict. It was a perfect site for us, for hard by was another considerable torrent and beside it we found Charles organising the pitching of the camp.

It had been a strenuous day but by no means an exhausting one. The most unpleasant feature for me had been the final descent, and for Charles and Frank the leeches. Charles who had pressed on heedlessly in his eagerness to get to the valley had been bitten quite severely and bled until late in the evening. To celebrate our arrival and our immediate proximity to the buru we opened one of our two bottles of brandy. That night, in one of his periodic fits of despondency, Charles began trying to convince himself that the buru would turn out to be a giant turtle. This would have been interesting enough zoologically, but it would have been by no means as sensational as a dinosaur. As Frank said, while Charles groaned: "It would be just too bad if the buru turned turtle!"

CHAPTER X

# First Day in Camp and First Reconnaissance

THE NEXT DAY ALL WAS HUSTLE AND BUSTLE IN THE CAMP.
We began with a pay parade, disposing of all the Lokra
Daflas, who turned back at once for home, and the hill
Daflas who scattered to their villages. With us remained
Orenimo, Pio Pio, Washington, the interpreters Taning and
Padme, and Tameng, the Apa Tani, who voluntarily
attached himself to us at this stage, and could not be per-
suaded to return home.

The Gurkha party, of whom another had fallen sick with
malaria, were to remain for two days to erect our permanent
quarters. These consisted of a table and three chairs in the
open; a wet weather basha, or hut, containing another table,
chairs and shelves; a roofed kitchen combined with servants'
quarters; a superior bathroom with floor of plaited bamboo,
and a latrine. We still used our tents for sleeping. The two
Daflas and Tameng, chiefly the latter, erected another basha
for their own use.

The whole we fenced round with rope to keep out the
mithan, or tame bison, which were already inquisitively
shambling round the camp in search of salt. These animals
are rare in that they cannot survive in the plains and are thus
never seen in captivity. They are never milked, but are used
for sacrificial purposes and represent wealth in the higher
brackets. Thus a comely virgin bride can be assessed in
value as worth, say, five mithan.

These mithan roam wild in the jungle round the villages
but never stray far, owing to the complete lack of salt, which
they soon learn can only be obtained from their owners. A

Dafla controls his mithan in exactly the same manner as a political officer controls his Daflas—by withholding salt!

We soon found that the mithan were tame enough to take salt from the hand but round the camp they were a menace and a danger to both huts and tents. A similar menace were the local domestic pigs, sharp snouted, their backs and shoulders covered with long stiff hair and their flanks and quarters gleaming black as if they had been gone over with stove polish. Kiro, the dog, soon proved he could take care of these.

Daflas from Rilo village had drifted into the camp the previous evening in twos and threes. They now came in scores and the exchange of presents with head-men and their numerous relations began. Out of the camp flowed pipes, leaf tobacco, cigarettes, hoe-heads and cups of rice spirit; into it flowed eggs carefully wrapped in nests of leaves, a scraggy chicken or two, pop-corn and gourds of rice beer. The most appreciated present we disposed of was the lens of a broken pocket-torch.

During this ceremony three headmen were present. Two of them, Tagora and Pinji of the neighbouring villages of Limdung Mundung and Chemgung had accompanied us from the plains. Both were sophisticated, having made many visits to Lokra, but while Pinji was comparatively harmless, Tagora was a perfect pest. He was a spry, agile old man of no dignity and little authority; a toady of the worst description who incessantly wheedled and cajoled for additional gifts. The third headman was Dodum of Rilo. Dodum delayed his appearance until the morning was well advanced; this was contrary to customary etiquette which demanded that he should have been one of our first visitors during the evening before. But Dodum wished it to be clearly understood we were not welcome. He had never been to the plains himself; he apparently darkly suspected that the real purposes of our visit was to depose him from authority, probably for some past misdemeanour of which we knew nothing. He stood apart, a middle-aged man of above medium height, tugging nervously at a straggling chin beard, the expression of anxiety on his face vying with one of curiosity as to our equipment and gear with particular reference to that portion of the presents which was to be his by right of his position.

After another round of rice-spirit, which nearly laid the insatiable Tagora flat on his back, we organised a sick-parade. No doctor has ever been appointed to the Dafla area in spite of its immense extent, nor have the tribe the use of a travelling dispensary such as have been established in other remote frontier areas. Thus every European entering the district, for whatever purpose, is saddled with the additional task of acting as jungle doctor. This custom was well known to Charles and consequently his medicine chest was bulging with every conceivable medicament and remedy. I watched him deal with infinite patience with a wide variety of cases ranging from the gaping gangrenous leg wound of a small girl who had been struck with a dao in a child's game, to the scarcely perceptible pimple of a strapping great warrior. Skin diseases were by far the most common ailment. The Dafla has no protection against dim-dam bites; he never washes but scratches himself incessantly, so it is no wonder that in time the exposed portions of his body, chiefly the thigh and calf, become covered with rashes of boils and ulcers which no single application of ointment can possibly cure.

To us also came a number of women who pointed to their swollen feet and complained of much pain. They looked at us in shocked surprise, however, and flatly refused to comply, when we suggested that they should take off the tightly wound ankle bands, which were the obvious cause of the trouble.

The afternoon closed with an impromptu archery exhibition, for the Daflas are great bowmen and never miss an opportunity to display their skill. For target, Frank produced a sheet of paper eight inches by six upon which he had pencilled a bull about two inches across. This paper he placed thirty feet up a tree about thirty-five yards from the camp. After a number of youths had carefully drawn their bows and narrowly missed the target, an elderly brave, hearing that a packet of cigarettes was to be won, slipped an arrow from his cane quiver, glanced along it, fitted it to the bow-string and taking apparently casual aim, struck the target about two inches from the bull. At the time, he was standing about five yards behind the mark, and did not even bother to toe the line. A second, younger brave, after two aiming shots which were near misses, released a third arrow which hit the dead centre of the bull! With the competition threatening to become expensive, we called a halt, and Frank, who had been thinking of giving an exhibition with the Mauser, quietly put the weapon back in its case.

Interrogation was not neglected that day, and although we found none who had seen the buru during the present season, all claimed to have seen it numbers of times in the past, and none could be shaken from the description of its appearance and habits which Charles had noted down during his original questioning. The general opinion was that it was due to appear any day.

The following morning, Frank being busy with the films and "dope-sheets" he wished the Gurkhas to take back to Lokra, Charles and I could no longer restrain our impatience to visit the buru swamp. Accordingly, after breakfast, we set out with the headman Pinji, Taning and Padme our two interpreters, and the faithful Tameng. We left our shelf, dropping down through a narrow belt of jungle and two enclosures stockaded against mithan, to the floor of the valley. This proved very pleasant going. Beneath the clumps of elephant grass and cane grew a rich carpet of white violets, mint and other tiny bog plants. Waist high stood wild raspberry bushes, their golden berries on the point of ripening. Veining the valley floor ran a number of tiny brooks and rivulets to be crossed by, at the most, a span of two slender poles, until they all converged in the main stream over which a good firm foot-bridge had been built. The ground here was soggy, but sound enough. At times we passed mithan, black, white and pie-bald, standing hock deep in lush grass, raising their heads curiously as we passed. The warm air was vibrant with the hum of insects, the shrilling of crickets and the croaking of frogs. Gaily coloured butterflies, as big as scallop shells, fluttered about us.

Beyond the main bridge the ground rose steeply upwards. We had reached the north-west corner of the valley and it turned out that we were climbing a spur of mountain which jutted out from the northern wall and enclosed the Buru Swamp between itself and the western barrier. The neck of the swamp lay open to the main valley floor to the south. For convenience I named this spur Lookout Hill. It was a stiff climb up the hill between walls of dense jungle but on this, the last lap, we stormed upwards until we were soaked in perspiration. The climb brought us abruptly to a broad swathe which had been cut down from the summit of the spur nearly to the swamp's edge.

This swathe had been formerly cultivated but had been left derelict and was now again considerably overgrown. It provided, however, a good over-all view of the swamp, and that view brought us up with our first shock. The swamp which we had imagined from the account of the Dafla at the Lenko camp, would by now be a broad lake, contained no open water at all! No water, that is, except two small pools each about twenty yards long and ten across, about thirty yards apart, at right angles to each other and two-thirds of the way towards the northern end of the swamp. From our observation point the pools were distant about seven hundred yards.

I could see that Charles was quite as taken aback as myself by the absence of water, but grimly he got out his huge telescope and began focusing it on the pools.

My own glasses could not compete with the telescope, and being no zoologist I confined myself to working out the mechanics of reaching the pools. All that remained of the swamp, which before silting occurred must have covered the entire valley, was an oblong some 1200 yards by 700 yards wide. The two pools, obviously at the lowest level, were surrounded by a two-hundred-yard-wide circle of brilliant emerald green marsh. About this circle was a band of light-brown withered grass, most of which appeared "laid" by flood or rain. This band was very irregular along its outer edge, but had an average width of about one hundred and fifty yards. The rest of the valley, to the jungle which came right down to swamp level, was filled in with tall reeds, liberally sprinkled, towards the southern end, with alder trees.

The process of flooding, should it occur, was quite obvious. Firstly, the two pools would join; then water would cover the patch of bright green which would provide the deepest and longest lying water; then water would spread over the band of withered sedge. This would form the lake proper. The eventual depth of water among the fringe of reeds would be questionable as it would remain invisible, but it might become as much as a foot.

Across the neck of the valley meandered the main Rilo stream, marked for the whole of its length by a dense serpentine of vegetation, until it disappeared in the gorge which was now hidden from us by a fold in the western mountain barrier. Two-thirds of the way across the neck, in a clump of trees, the stream appeared to be joined by a narrow tributary which wound its way into the swamp and might possibly have its source in the two visible pools. This was guess-work, as from where I was looking at it, it was impossible to judge either width or depth, or even the continuity of the tributary.

Somehow we had to conquer the inaccessibility of the swamp and as I saw it then, there were two ways of reaching

the pools. Either we could cut out way down through the
jungle to the nearest point on shore and thence build a
bamboo causeway, which would be laborious but by no
means impossible. We could, of course, shorten the labour
by merely building two bamboo ladders, leap-frogging the
one over the other across the swamp, but in that case, should
the buru turn out to be more formidable than we thought
it was and round on us in pursuit, the line of retreat would
be ludicrously precarious!

Or, we could use one of our rubber boats, float downstream to the clump of trees, and then paddle up the tributary, providing it was there, into the heart of the swamp. At
first sight this looked a very pleasurable outing, but there
were a number of drawbacks. Firstly, although the stream
at the footbridge was broad and deep enough to float a boat,
there was no knowing what was behind even the first bend.
We might well find ourselves hacking our way for hundreds
of yards; there would be bound to be fallen logs to negotiate;
bound also to be submerged snags to watch for, and the
farther we got into the swamp the less I relished the idea
of a pneumatic boat suddenly deflating beneath me. The
boat excursion, therefore, began to assume the proportions
of a Commando operation. The entire trip might well take
two days, including a night spent in the swamp. I did not
abandon the plan, but intended to produce it as a last resort.
After all, given ideal conditions, water and a boat was as
sound a way as any of reaching the buru.

All this time Charles's well-moulded forehead had been
puckered over the eye-piece of the telescope. He finally
interrupted my thoughts by asking my opinion as to what
I could see in the pools. Seen through the telescope, the
aspect of the water was constantly changing owing to passing clouds and occasional light puffs of wind, but, taking
this into account, it was impossible to escape from the
fact that every now and then there appeared to be an additional disturbance which had its centre round an object of

indefinable shape, but brown in colour, which lay at the end of the first pool. From that range one could not identify the object as a living creature unless it made a more definite move; it might merely be a submerged mud-bank. It was, of course, quite invisible to the naked eye.

Upon the alarm being translated to Pinji he seized the glasses, rapidly twisted them completely out of focus and announced a large brown animal with long neck and horns! This completely disgusted Charles.

Nevertheless, Charles had seen what I had seen and our confidence, which had been drained from us when we had first viewed the empty swamp, welled once more.

Further observation that afternoon produced nothing more definite, and as the sky was clouding over we packed up for the day. One further thing of interest we had all seen. To the south, at a bend of the stream, had appeared two grazing mithan. They were about 700 yards away; the distance at which most of the Daflas had seen the buru. To us, the mithan appeared as nothing more than a vague mass; for the Daflas to have made out "a head like an ox with a long snout and horns" on the buru emphasised the fact that it must be an animal of considerable bulk.

That evening, over our sundown tot of rice spirit and ginger beer we thought out our course of action. The first move was to find a vantage point much nearer the pools, so that we could establish without doubt that there was something within them as both Charles and I then thought. The next step was to get to the pools, either by bamboo causeway or by the stream.

Speed was essential, for our best chance of success would be gone once the pools joined and the water spread over a wider area. It was to be a race against the rain. If we could establish a firm platform beside one of the pools there was no reason why we should not get a rope, or better two, round whatever was swimming there, haul it out on the bank, examine it at leisure, film it and then turn it loose. We were no longer so keen on killing one of the animals, for when we had suggested such a thing to the three headmen they had shaken their heads and pronounced that such an act would certainly bring disaster to someone. The scowling Dodum had actually looked horrified. With an epidemic about in the surrounding villages, and the possibility of further deaths among the Daflas coinciding with the slaying of a buru, we simply could not afford to take the risk.

That night, however, we went to bed happy in the thought that we had a programme that would keep us occupied for a week at least.

# CHAPTER XI

# Into the Swamp

THE NEXT MORNING SAW US EARLY ON LOOKOUT HILL. WE reached our observation point of the day before and there divided forces. Charles and Tameng went on down the slope and we could soon hear Tameng hack-thwacking about with his dao in the thicket which separated the foot of the clearing from the swamp. Frank and I continued along the brow of the hill with the exuberant Taning and his fellow interpreter Padme, to carry the cameras. We were also joined by two local Dafla striplings who had been hunting green pigeon with bows and arrows and now joined in to see the fun.

We soon reached the end of the cleared swathe and the edge of the jungle, but to our delight a good path led on upward through the trees. The swamp was now completely out of sight, but we were walking parallel to it and relied on our ability to judge when we should come opposite the two pools. When we guessed we had reached this point we turned off down through the jungle. At first the going was easy, though steep; the trees were well spaced and the undergrowth none too dense. A number of game trails zig-zagged across the slope and by using these we made good progress. Soon, however, the undergrowth grew darker and denser, and the gradient plunged downwards abruptly. Here the Daflas who had been setting the pace and cutting the way, began to dawdle. One of the local youths swung himself into a tree, climbed rapidly upwards, and then announced that there was no point going farther as he could see the swamp clearly and there was nothing in it. This vantage point was of no use to me as I could not possibly climb the tree with one hand; nor was it of any use to Frank as we were still well out of camera range. Therefore we ordered an advance. The Daflas, however, hung back and produced a variety of excuses. First, the gradient was too steep; then the undergrowth was too thick and would cause too much labour; then we should all get very wet; then we shall all get very dirty, and who would clean the trousers of Taning and Padme?

Finally it all came out; we had reached a haunt of Evil Spirits! At this there was nothing for it, but for Frank and I to lead the way. This looked a forlorn hope, as for cutting through the undergrowth my heavy cane walking-stick was of as much use as a cricket bat. Cursing, sliding, bending under fallen trees, forcing our way between the close-growing bamboo stems we made some sort of headway, but the pair of us were soon gasping and bathed in perspiration. I was about to give up when we were suddenly joined by Taning, more subdued than I have ever known him. This happily started a stampede; it was obviously considered better to stick close to the Sahibs than to be left alone, a sacrifice to the spirits!

The party complete once more, with its vanguard of vigorously swung daos, made light of the rest of the descent and with no further delay we reached the rim of the swamp. Here, I could scarcely blame the Daflas, for we had come to a fœtid, noisesome place. The canopy of foliage above us completely shut out the light and through the gloom we stumbled on over a dank bed of rotting leaves and branches, occasionally splashing through stagnant, scum-covered pools of water. From the centre of the swamp we were shut off by a hundred-yard belt of reeds woven together by a thick mat of eight-foot-high dried grass, berberis and a shrub which emitted a pungent aniseed aroma when crushed. Visibility was nil. To remedy this we chose a tree, and by cutting notches in the trunk, soon had Frank in a position whence he could view the swamp. But although he could make out the central patch of emerald green, we had come too low for him to have any clear view of the pools. Impatient and helpless on the ground, while Frank dangled his legs aloft and announced the familiar landmarks like a guide in a charabanc, I then turned towards the swamp. There was no question of there being any firm holding underfoot, but by treading down the grass into a compact carpet it was quite possible to make some progress. Choosing the youngest and smallest Dafla, with a dao no bigger than a kitchen knife, I managed to bully him into accompanying me, and together we trod out a path through the grass about twenty yards long. At that point the ground began to shiver beneath us, and try as I would I could not persuade the Dafla to go farther. So we returned to Frank. In my own mind I was decided that we could still go a long way without risking any more than a ducking, for with so much vegetation about it would be impossible to sink out of sight, but as, for him, the Dafla had already performed a prodigious feat of fortitude, I let him off. He was witless beyond belief for a jungle-bred boy and in a moment of idle curiosity had nearly cut a hornet's nest in half.

It was now past noon and we were undecided what to do next, when we heard a distant "Hallo" from Charles about whom we were becoming anxious. Ten minutes more brought him to us. He had had an appallingly exhausting morning. He and Tameng had done well until they had reached the edge of the swamp. They had then come to a grove of young alders through which they had had to hack their way yard by yard. Tameng had finally given up spent and sobbing for breath. Charles had replaced him with the dao, and taking turn, and turn about they had at last fought their way through to clearer ground. But they had got no nearer the pools than we had.

After a quick lunch Charles tried my path through the grass, and at once agreed with me that it could be pushed a good deal farther. Charles stood no nonsense with the

Daflas and soon Taning and the Apa Tani, Tameng, were competing with each other for the honour of leading the way. The grass they laid by flinging their bodies on to it, and pressing it to the ground.

With Frank directing operations from his perch in the tree, it was not long before the rest of us had beaten our way through the reed belt, and stood in the open swamp surveying the green patch from a distance of a mere hundred yards. But we were still not near enough to have an adequate sight of the pools. Before us stretched a belt of knee-high clumps of sedge standing in black, stagnant water. The whole of this area quaked and quivered alarmingly as soon as we tested it. However, two hundred yards to the left, and much nearer the centre of the swamp, grass such as that through which we had come, appeared to reach almost to the edge of the green patch. This point was our next objective, and while the Daflas remained forlornly behind, not daring to venture farther, Charles and I set off, skirting the grass and stepping quickly to avoid breaking through the crust.

Some minutes of walking through the swamp without mishap made us bolder and when we reached the green we turned off into it. We found that the vivid colour, almost dazzling when seen through the telescope, was due to a thick carpet of dwarf ferns and rushes which appeared to grow nowhere else. This carpet sagged ominously under our weight but by keeping on the move we found that water seldom rose above our calves. We were so low in the swamp that it was sometime before we could locate the pools. It was in floundering towards them that we made the discovery which brought us up stock still, regardless of the fact that we were sinking so that marsh gas was soon bubbling about our knees. Quite distinct, before us, were the tracks of a four-footed beast! Each mark was water-filled and impossible to register by plaster cast, but they were undoubtedly those of a large, heavy animal. In that ridiculous

7

position, with the carpet beneath us threatening to give way at any moment and drop us through to Eternity, we stood grinning cheerfully at each other and composing a succinct cable to London after the manner of Edward Malone, the journalist of *The Lost World*: "There is life in the Buru Swamp!"

Closer inspection showed that though we had first come on the tracks of a solitary animal there was a regular trail connecting the two pools. Moreover, along this trail the plants on either side had been nipped and bruised by a browsing beast. There were also at least two patches of crushed fern where some large animal had lain and rolled. At that moment I believe that both Charles and I thought we had merely to reach the pools to solve once and for all the mystery of the buru. Heedless of danger, the pair of us made for the nearest pool. Then the inevitable happened. The ground under Charles, who was a little ahead of me and to one side, gave one final shudder and sank, and he was in up to the waist. Almost at the same instant I had felt the ground giving beneath me, and before I could do anything to rescue Charles or save myself I, too, was down. For a brief moment I thought that the buru expedition was coming to an abrupt end there and then, but both of us were saved by our sticks of stout cane which the Daflas had cut for us at Takko Senyak. By laying these across the carpet, and heaving, and floundering for a minute or two both of us managed to get back on our feet. That was the first physical effort I had made since my accident in which I entirely forgot the pain of my shoulder!

When this mishap occurred we had approached to within five yards of the pool, but neither of us had any stomach left for a second attempt. We were, however, both agreed that there could scarcely be enough free water then present to support an aquatic beast of any size. What, then, could be the explanation of the footprints? We were not long in finding out. Treading a deal sight more gingerly than we had done hitherto we made our way back to firmer ground. And there, while we were still well in the middle of the patch of green, we made the discovery which dashed all our hopes and set us right back once more at our starting-point. Unconsciously we had been following the tracks of the animal whose trail we had first sighted. A few yards of sounder ground now showed these tracks to be nothing more than those of a deer! Not only were the slot marks well-defined; droppings soon established the identity of the animal beyond doubt. So this particular "buru" was nothing more than a Sambhar, or possibly a large swamp deer! With that, all our elation departed, and for the first time we felt the clammy unpleasantness of our soaked clothes.

Back by the grass we were joined by the Daflas, all mightily pleased with themselves for they had achieved immortality by being the first of their kind to brave the terrors of the swamp. After them, floundered Frank, pleased not at all, for his heavier weight caused him to sink down above the knee at each step. Tamang, too, had one nasty moment when his slender form disappeared up to his chest.

Gathered on firmish ground in the centre of the swamp, there was no point in making for the nearest shore and climbing up and down Look-out Hill again. So in Indian file, with no word spoken, we squelched up to the stream at the neck of the swamp, and thence, by a little used trail, to the main valley path. Silently, we turned off towards the camp; silently we sat at the open-air tea-table massaging our crumpled toes while Tameng, with no spare nettle-cloth garment to change into, squatted over the fire.

How long this mood of despondency would have lasted I cannot say, had it not been relieved somewhat that evening by the arrival of a brave from Rilo village. This man, whom we had not seen before, was of well above average intelligence and had great sobriety of expression. He laughed heartily when we charged him that the buru was nothing more than a deer. No, the buru was certainly not a deer.

Everyone knew there were deer in the swamp. Besides, who ever heard of a deer that bobbed up and down in the water at high noon when the sun was brightest. The buru was quite a different animal; too common to merit any special comment. He himself had seen them many times, so had a great number of braves and the women who work in the fields. They appeared when the sun was at its height, and there was much water in the swamp. They rose to this height (raising his arm to shoulder level), remained up one minute and then sank (resting his fingers on the ground).

This description heartened us, for it tallied in every detail with what we had heard before. Either all the Daflas were liars, or we had to accept the fact that there was still a buru to be found.

None the less, it was now necessary to revise our ideas considerably, and to scrap our programme of the previous night.

As regards the Daflas, it hardly seemed credible that they could be the victims of mass hallucination regarding what was to them a common enough object to which they attached no religious, or other special significance. The western slope bordering the swamp, at least, showed signs of intensive cultivation. Broad bands of jungle had been cleared upon it, the trees felled and scattered haphazard down the hillside. In at least three places field-huts had been erected with a clear view of the swamp. Thus a large number of Daflas had been in a position whence they could have seen the buru or could not, and so far the "Ayes" vastly exceeded the "Noes". There was no question of the swamp being in an isolated, little visited, spot; had this been so there might well have been room for doubt.

Concerning the buru, if we were to believe the Daflas, we could now rule out the deer theory, as well as the crocodile. The giant turtle seemed to rule itself out, for taking into account the nature of the swamp, it would be bound to move out of it to lay its eggs and somewhere, at some time, it must have been seen by somebody. A huge lung fish seemed most improbable, for no known fish would expose itself above water, for no practical purpose, for such a length of time. The giant newt was still a possibility, but whether we would or no, the animal we were drawing nearest to, by process of elimination, was the strange beast of the Apa Tani tradition; a creature that "lived on the mud", craned its neck sometimes above the weeds, and never came to land. At Rilo there was mud aplenty, for judging by the angle at which the mountain slopes hit the level of the swamp, the depth in the centre could well be hundreds of feet.

At the same time, we were beginning to doubt whether the final extent of open water at the height of the rains would ever be anything like as great as we had first imagined. It was more reasonable now to suppose that as the level of the water rose, in most areas the floating carpet of weeds and plants would rise with it.

We scrapped our programme because, having walked all over the swamp, there was no need for further reconnaissance. We had found out that probably at all seasons we should be able to get an appreciable distance towards the pools, and from that point we could construct our bamboo causeway with, if necessary, a look-out post at the end of it, using the boats as pontoons. All that remained was to sit back and wait for the buru to make its first undeniable appearance. For this purpose our first observation post on Lookout Hill was adequate, for from it we could cover the whole area of the swamp with our glasses.

We closed our council of war in a sober frame of mind. Not even Frank had a quip or wisecrack to lighten the occasion. It was to be no picnic after all.

The buru had won the first round; if we were finally to run him to ground and solve the mystery there was hard work in plenty ahead.

# CHAPTER XII

# The Village

THE NEXT DAY WAS A WASHOUT FOR IT RAINED INCESSANTLY, but it was marked by a notable encounter. We were seated in the basha after breakfast, preparing the mail bags for Lokra and listening to the rain drumming on the tarpaulin roof, when suddenly the entrance was blocked by a truly splendid figure of a man. He was a shade under six feet in height, deep-chested, with wide shoulders and beautifully muscled limbs. His features were strong and regular, the head well set, the eyes unflinching. Everything about his dress and accoutrements denoted care of choice and wealth such as few hill Daflas could hope to achieve. In his cane cap was set the feather of an eagle instead of that of the more customary hornbill; his garment was of good black cloth traded in from the plains; his dao, the largest I ever saw, was hung round his neck on a thin gilt chain; his necklaces and ornaments were many in number, and told a story of noble ancestry. But it was his poise, carriage and dignity which stamped him as a man far superior to his fellows. Standing with arms akimbo he at once embarked on a long monologue delivered in grave tones. He spoke in Dafla, heedless that it was obvious that none of us could follow him; plainly it was his attitude that it was our business to understand, not his to explain. Taning was hastily summoned and listened half-incredulous. At length he turned to us and we learned what it was all about.

We were speaking to Tapook, younger brother of the headman Dodum. He had come to claim damages from us for bamboo cut on the far side of Lookout Hill during our excursion of the day before. All bamboo on that side of the swamp, asserted Tapook, belonged to him. It was an offence to cut it without his permission, but since it had been done we must make good the loss.

This was such a fantastic claim that Charles, in some anger, dismissed it at once. Clumps of cultivated bamboo grew all over the valley; the villagers had merely to walk a hundred yards or so from their houses to ensure their entire requirements for years to come. No man in his senses, and certainly no Dafla, would walk nearly two miles with a stiff climb at the end of them to obtain that which he might cut outside his own doorstep. Besides, the bamboos growing by the swamp were thin, weakly and of poor quality where they were not already dead and rotting. Charles, therefore, announced that no damages would be paid.

Tapook received this news with a slight flicker of the eyes. He then opened his pouch, produced a brand new briar pipe which we had given one of his companions two days before, filled it with two of our cigarettes also from the pouch, and lit it with steel and firestone. After two or three defiant puffs, as much as to say: "Very well, if you will give me nothing directly, you may be sure I shall find some means of getting it indirectly," he strode off into the jungle.

We debated this incident for some time. As Charles said, it was conceivable that Tapook would journey to the plains, and lay his complaint before the Political Officer, possibly to strengthen his case for the redressment of some more genuine grievance. We did not wish to gain an unjust reputation for mishandling the tribes, so forthwith Charles sat down and wrote a brief note to Menzies explaining our side of the affair. Our own impression, formed on the spur of the moment was, however, that Tapook, in spite of his magnificent appearance, must be a trifle simple-minded. How deeply we wronged him! We soon learned that Tapook did nothing without first deliberating his move for hours beforehand. After we had come to know the working of the Tapook mind it became easier to explain his initial conduct towards us. He had missed the original distribution of presents; why, we never found out. He was too proud to beg; too parsimonious to barter. Some method must be found to place us in his debt without costing himself anything. Hence the bamboo. This was a clumsy ruse; his next move, however, was both ingenious and unexpected.

That afternoon a horde of small boys descended on the camp, and spent an uproarious hour cavorting and gambolling about, turning cart-wheels, pole-jumping and long-jumping, and firing tiny arrows into the air. Some time after we discovered that the ringleaders in this entertainment were Tapook's own merry little son Ria, and Dodum's boy Senyak, and that their entire earnings in boiled sweets and cigarettes found their way into the Tapook pouch. Thereafter Tapook became a permanent fixture about the camp. He bore us no grudge. Hour after hour he would sit on the bench by the kitchen hut, solemnly smoking his pipe and pondering heaven knows what. Gravely he would accept any presents that came his way as being no more than his right, yet although he never offered us as much as an egg in return, and he was more hindrance than help to us, all of us grew very fond of him. It would, in fact, be impossible to imagine the camp without the inevitable Tapook.

The following morning broke fine again, and all three of us were up early and settled down on Lookout Hill.

Patches of sun and shade followed each other rapidly over the swamp; a dab-chick or teal was busy in the farthest pool, and once in a distant corner of the swamp we saw a sounder of pigs, so small at that range as to be almost beyond sight of the telescope. We saw no other sign of life all day. That evening we decided that there was no point in all three of us being on duty at the same time, and we agreed to stand watches; a forenoon watch from nine till one, an afternoon watch from one till four. This easy routine gave each of us a holiday every third day. We owed it to our sponsors to take this watch-keeping seriously. There were to be no lapses of

discipline such as all three of us being absent from the swamp
at the same time. We were to allow ourselves no conces-
sions, such as a day's hunting with the Daflas, until the Buru
had shown itself. Thus began a series of blank days.

The two of us who were off watch together invariably
found much to do. The Daflas were our main preoccupa-
tion. A man of Tapook's calibre and composure was very
much the exception rather than the rule. Every morning a
fresh party would arrive in the camp for medical treatment, or
to press for further gifts, or to arrange barter deals with
eggs, chickens and rice-beer. In turn we paid many visits to
Rilo village. This lay about half a mile from the camp along
the southern slope of the valley. One first crossed a belt of
jungle swamp cut by our own stream and a second, then
two enclosures wherein women and children were weeding
between the young rice and millet plants. The path then led
through a bramble thicket where grew delicious golden and
red raspberries. These raspberries were ignored by the
Daflas, but provided us with most tasty dessert dishes. This
was the only food we ever obtained from the Daflas without
hard bargaining.

The five houses of the village were clustered according to
no particular plan, and were set some distance apart from
each other. The first one we came to, that of the village cap-
maker, was on the near side of a deep gully which at the
height of the rains must have entirely separated it from the
other four. On the far side of the gully stood the Dodum
establishment beside a magnificent clump of bamboo. The
glum Dodum invariably watched our approach with mis-
givings for custom and courtesy demanded that we should
pause a while with him to drink rice-beer. His was the
largest house, and his the largest number both of dependants
and farm animals. Two fields away lived Tapook. Judging
by the care with which he dressed himself, we had imagined
that he would show the same pride over his house, but this
was very far from the case. It was a long low ruin of a place,

ill-kept and dilapidated. To add to the Tapook misfortunes, the entire central section had at one time caught fire, and now remained scorched and blackened as witness to the disaster.

The remaining two houses, in one of which lived Nana, the priest, lay together some distance to the west. Between them stood a low square table on which lounged the village notables when they were not off hunting in the jungle.

The table also served Nana as a dais for the performance of various public offices.

All houses had an open platform at both ends where visitors were received, and where the women performed such domestic tasks as pounding grain in hollowed sections of tree trunks. Each house also had its complement of chickens, pigs and goats, scavenging and scratching between the stilts and below the only floor, but the village as a whole smelt sweeter than anything I had experienced in India.

Beside each house stood the graves of deceased family members. Over each grave was erected a framework of woven sticks surmounted by a series of small effigies or dolls whittled from bamboo stems. A good deal of imagination was necessary to attribute any recognisable shape to the effigies, but they probably represented benignant spirits summoned to shield the departed soul on its journey to the next world. Also hung on the framework, were a cooking utensil, a drinking cup and an implement for cultivation in order that the dead man might be sufficiently provided for when he reached his journey's end.

Larger panels were erected to mark the sacrifice of a mithan. These panels were surmounted by a series of crude carvings on long poles. Some of these devices resembled wooden horns. Others were clearly meant to be birds on the wing, a device which occurs very frequently among tribes right across the Assam frontier and certainly as far as the Nungs of Burma.

It would be difficult to find any less sophisticated tribe than the Daflas. Although their country is geographically

contained within the frontiers of India, the vast majority
have never seen an Indian from the plains, let alone a white
man. Few, if any, have ever heard of Gandhi, or Nehru, or
any other Indian leader. They know no other law than
their own; recognise no authority other than that of their
village headman.

During our stay Charles, with the help of Taning, collected considerable data on the Daflas, and has permitted me
to make the following quotation from his notes:

"The Daflas are divided roughly into the Eastern and the
Western stocks. The Eastern branch (among whom we
were), are probably in the majority. They are extremely
primitive both in their organisation and their way of living,
in which they are far behind the Naga tribes. Thus, they do
not weave, have no art, virtually no blacksmiths or metal
working. Their cultivation is most rough and ready, and
the only craft is that of pot making. The Eastern Daflas live
in long communal houses, with no partitions, and a series of
hearths down the centre. A rich man's house may be over
two hundred feet long, and have twelve or more hearths.
Each hearth is the 'home' of a family, either of the owner's
relatives, or of his dependants. Up to two hundred and fifty
people are said to live in some of the bigger houses. The
Eastern Daflas build their villages widely scattered over
small ridges, and a village of fifteen long houses may cover
a square mile.

"The Western Daflas live in the same style, but their houses
are built close together in a compact village, are partitioned
off inside and are more solidly built. They all weave (from
nettle fibre), and do a fair amount of metal working.

"Cultivation is very rough and ready, and is essentially the
job of the women, while the men do little more than cut and
burn the forest each winter. Crops are rice, millet, maize, Job's
tears, sweet potatoes, oil-plant, yams. The millet is grown
mainly for beer-making. Very few vegetables are used, and
they rely mainly on jungle leaves, bamboo shoots, berries, etc.

"Mithan (*bos frontalis*), pigs, goats and fowls are kept in great numbers, the Daflas being great meat eaters. Consumption of livestock is closely linked with their use as sacrificial animals. Much more interest is taken in their mithan than in the crops.

"There is an elaborate system of internal trade, involving the perpetual circulation of mithan, Thibetan bells, necklaces of semi-precious stones, cloths, pigs and goats: all of which are really in the nature of currency. True money is used, but only to a limited extent. The bells and necklaces are valued according to individual characteristics, history and markings, and have a totally different system of values from those of our system.

"Polygamy is the normal custom and a man has wives according to his means, up to ten or twelve. The senior wife runs the house. Heavy marriage prices are paid of mithan, cloth, bells, etc. Often the contract is arranged and the price paid in part, while the girl is still a small child.

"Like all tribes of this region, the Daflas are animists, and believe in a great assembly of spirits, the greater number of which are evil, and have to be constantly propitiated by offerings to ward off disaster, cure sickness, etc. There is a well-established system of priests, who are called in to perform the ceremonies of sacrifice, and receive fees of money, cloth or meat, largely in proportion to the success or otherwise of their efforts in curing the sickness. As a preliminary to each ceremony, the priests take omens by examining the yoke of an egg, to decide on the nature of the sacrifice, and which spirit has been offended, or has to be propitiated. This decides whether mithan, pigs, fowls or goats are to be killed. Among the Western Daflas at least, an elaborate ritual accompanies the killing of a mithan, and oddly made wooden carvings are put up in honour of the spirits to whom the sacrifice is offered. Among the principal gods is the sun, which is regarded as female. Certain trees, pools, rocks, etc. are regarded as the homes of evil spirits.

"Before the present loose administration started, raids were very frequent, and the raiders killed or captured everyone possible. Raids were due to feuds over debts, or jealousies. A common cause of a raid was 'sickness-carrying'—an epidemic in one village would be attributed to the disease being introduced by a man from another village, and the former would take retribution from the alleged 'carrier' village.

"A man captured in a raid became the servant of his captor and lives in his house. A common practice was to cut off the right hand of a man killed in battle and bury it.

"Daflas are great hunters, going out in small parties, with their own breed of small dogs. All game is killed, although it is considered unlucky to kill a Sambhar deer. For hunting, poisoned arrows are used: the poison is vegetable and made partly from aconite roots, traded in from higher, colder regions."

*Note.*—(The following extract from the travels of the Jesuit Desideri in Thibet in the early eighteenth century refers to the extreme Eastern Daflas and the Abors:

"These Lhoba (southern people) are proud, uncultured and wild. They generally live in the forests and shoot wild animals with bows and arrows, which they eat raw, or half-roasted. Occasionally they devour human flesh and do not hesitate to kill a man when he is young, fat and of good complexion. They always go armed with bows and arrows and are admirable shots. A most barbarous custom prevails among them. When a man is dying some of his relations console him by telling him not to be cast down or afraid of being left alone when he leaves this world, because they will send so many companions (specifying the number) to comfort him with their conversation. As soon as he is dead these relations or friends kill the number of persons promised, and as token that the promise has been fulfilled they make a necklace of a number of teeth corresponding to the number of persons they have slaughtered."

This account is based entirely on hearsay from Thibet. The allegation of cannibalism is certainly untrue; the sentences concerning human sacrifice may well have been correct).—R. I.

CHAPTER XIII

# In the Camp

IN CAMP THE BLANK DAYS PASSED PLEASANTLY ENOUGH. WE
were at such an altitude that the days were comfortably warm
and the nights cold enough for a log fire and a couple of
blankets. We rose each morning at five-thirty for without a
hasty application of repellent oil soon after sunrise, dim-
dam flies made life intolerable. Dim-dam flies were the
main drawback. Unfortunately for me I proved especially
allergic to them, and for days at a time my hands and wrists
remained puffed and swollen so that it became painful to
grasp anything. Both Charles and Frank were bitten, but
not with such severe effect; the stalwart Frank actually spent
many of the sunshine hours stripped to the waist. Shaving
and washing in the morning was a hasty affair; bathing was
delayed until evening when we had only mosquitoes to con-
tend with. We defeated these by pouring oil on the bath
water, taking care not to emerge naked beyond the protect-
ing pillar of citronella scented steam.

By eight-thirty a.m. one of us would invariably be off on
his way to the swamp accompanied either by Taning, Padme
or Tameng. Each of us found plenty to do in his spare time.
I began writing this narrative; Frank pottered happily with
his camera; Charles occupied hours in the village making
notes and bartering for chickens or a pig. We never
achieved the pig. Later on it became apparent that each
individual animal was already earmarked for some forthcoming transaction with a neighbouring village. I, for one,
was not particularly sorry. In a Dafla village the pig is the
great eater of refuse, and fills much the role of a septic tank in
a more civilised community. Orenimo roamed the clearing

searching for edible fungi and wild spinach, crooning to himself and knitting a succession of woollen socks for Charles. The Daflas dammed the stream, built a bathing pool and constructed two unproductive fish traps. Tameng erected over his quarters a mast from which depended a cigarette tin lid on a long piece of string. The lid spun in the wind and was meant to drive away evil spirits, but it proved a ready target for the Dafla archers who shot it down so frequently that Tamang finally tired of putting it up again and dared the spirits to possess him. Pio Pio, the second Naga boy, went down with malaria but quickly recovered. Washington kept his own counsel, but continued to produce a good variety of dishes from the same essential ingredients. Neither Washington, nor Pio Pio, nor Orenimo ever left the clearing. Having no interest in the buru none of them had much inducement to do so, for as soon as one stepped from the beaten path into the dank shade of the jungle the battle with leeches began once more.

There were many snakes in the jungle, particularly in the swampy patches, but it was some time before we were troubled with them in the camp. However, one morning I discovered a small viper in the latrine pit. This was dispatched by Orenimo who hooked it out on the end of a stick and flung it into the cooking fire where it writhed in agony until I knocked its head off with the wood-chopper. There was a good deal of the savage still left in Orenimo. In the patch of marsh just below the clearing we discovered two varieties which none of us could name. The first was copper brown with bands of iridescent violet and the second brown, with thin bars of black. Both appeared to average about thirty inches in length. The second variety was found by Charles and me in circumstances which might have been unpleasant. We had gone for an evening stroll together when Charles paused to point out a rare and beautiful flower. At the same moment I pointed out the snake coiled about six inches from his ankle. I achieved by far the more spectacular effect!

In this swamp, too, we came upon what we believe to be a new variety of raspberry. Certainly Charles, in his many wanderings in the Assam hills, had never come across it before. It was a bush plant, growing roughly waist-high. It was in fruit, and the circular berries, well over an inch in diameter, glowed like so many scarlet Chinese lanterns. We pulped the fruit carefully in water; dried the seed in the sun and brought some home to England where it is now germinating furiously.

We whiled away many an interesting hour in the clearing itself. It was studded with stumps where trees had been cut down at hip height. These stumps harboured many fat beetle grubs which are eaten by the Daflas as a delicacy with which to flavour their rice. The grubs were, of course, vegetable fed and thus contained no inedible matter; even a Dafla draws the line at an earth fed grub!

The rotting trunks of the felled trees provided the source whence Orenimo procured his fungi. We soon learned which were edible—Jew's Ear Fungus was the most prolific —and we collected ourselves for the fun of it, but Orenimo always insisted on making the final selection himself before any went into the cooking pot.

We also began a collection of insect oddities for which Tameng wove an intricate specimen box from whittled down slats of bamboo. Charles started the ball rolling by bringing in the most perfect leaf-insect I have ever seen. It was identical in shape, size and colour with a full-grown green beech leaf. Each limb was an unfurled leaf, and so true was the camouflage, even down to a blight spot or two and brown stain round the fringe, that only an expert eye could have spotted it. We combed the clearing thoroughly but never found another. We did, however, capture a giant stick insect, like a miniature animated bassoon, and Frank contributed a six-inch long furry caterpillar which sparkled like a bejewelled armband. This caterpillar wrapped itself in a cocoon in its compartment in the box, and later emerged as a beautiful moth with wings of canary coloured velvet. My own find was a flat praying mantis almost as big as my hand. This was another wonderful lesson in natural camouflage for it was mottled like a piece of lichen covered bark. I should never have seen it on the tree trunk where it lay had I not nearly sat on it. All these insects came to a horrible end as I shall relate.

Glorious orchids grew in abundance on trees round the clearing. Many hung high above the ground but some nimble climbing by Tameng soon recovered for us a number of varieties, one of which was more like a delicate iris and was very sweet smelling. These we hung in natural and more accessible positions round the camp, for Frank badly wanted some shots of orchids for his colour film. He was up to every trick of flower photography, and during filming Charles fanned the blossoms with a newspaper to produce a breeze effect, while I sprinkled them with water from a kerosene can to endow them with dew-drops. During this performance Frank would keep up a travelogue commentary as follows: "It was a valley of glorious orchids—but the fairest orchid of all was the headman's daughter, had she but painted her lips instead of her teeth!" In one effect only did we appear faced with failure. Frank was insistent that he must have the stock shot of an insect settling on a flower. For a full half hour we stood by idly whistling for insects to appear. None came. The deadlock was solved by Orenimo. Approaching with the air of mute inquiry he reserved for situations when he sensed the Sahibs at a loss, he sized up the problem, retired and returned once more with a substance which he smeared on the petals. This was miraculously effective and soon all the handsome insects we could wish for were buzzing round the flowers and alighting upon them. When questioned about his magic elixir, which had given us a perfect picture, Orenimo collapsed into chuckles and giggles. It was a distinct anti-climax later to learn that the substance was nothing more romantic than mithan

8

dung! Orenimo was a practical young man; there was a trick or two up his sleeve which not even Frank had up till then included in his repertoire.

With butterflies we were less successful. Their numbers and the variety of their size and colours were a constant source of delight and amazement to us. Thumbing through my diary I have come across such notes as: "falling like flakes from the blue dome of the sky": "a scrap of blue enamel": "a fragment of crimson damask": "lavender—dark wine—damson—sulphur—a blue-green flash—pure turquoise": but no words of mine can adequately describe them. We found that they settled most readily on the moist patch of flattened earth where we drew our water from the stream, and on similar patches on either side of the gully down in the village. These offered the safest drinking and possibly a thin film of salt left by the passage of so many bare-feet. But try as we would we could never get them to settle long enough with opened wings to get a satisfactory close-up. Particularly elusive were the great, many-hued swallow-tails. These gave the illusion of being cumbersome on the wing, but in reality they propelled themselves with surprising agility backwards as well as forwards, up or down.

Apart from the waterside, they swarmed in great numbers far above our heads about the flowers which blossomed on the summits of the tallest trees. In desperation we chose a huge Albizzia Lebbek, which grew near the camp, and which was crowned with a creamy foam of flowers and set Taning, Tameng and the Daflas to felling it. It took them the better part of a morning with their daos and when the giant finally came crashing down we were appalled at the damage we had wrought. But although the butterflies came down with the flowers they immediately swarmed back again to the heights, and we left the great tree rotting, its flowers browning, dead and untasted.

Out at the swamp things remained unchanged. Right from the early days of watch-keeping there was a good deal more rain than sunshine, and consequently the water-level appeared to rise slightly, but there was still no buru.  Occasionally we saw a pig; sometimes we heard the baying of hunting dogs from the village of Chemgung which lay over the lip of the western slope of the swamp.  These dogs were foot-high, half-tame, foxy-faced creatures who reputedly would put up deer, python, pig or tortoise with equal abandon.  Once or twice the clamour of the hunt was audible from dawn till dusk as it trailed endlessly up one mountain and down another.  It was this seemingly interminable pursuit, through staggeringly difficult country, which, quite apart from the leeches, dissuaded us from asking permission to join in a chase.  Thus, I have never been "capped" by Dodum, and an article, "A day with the Rilo hounds", which I had intended to submit to the editor of *Horse and Hound*, will never be written.

Only once did we hear the high-pitched, intermittent wails of triumph, at first faint from afar, then louder as they approached the village, which denoted that there had been a kill and fresh meat for all was at hand.

Throughout those early, happy days, our faith in the buru remained unshaken.  With aid of Taning and Padme we carried out scores of interrogations until the Daflas began to become restive under repeated questionings.  By this time we had a perfect word-picture; the problem was, "How to improve upon it?"  One morning the idea occurred to me that numbers of Daflas could draw the buru blindfold, if they could draw, which of course they could not.  But what if I were to teach a Dafla to draw; surely that would provide an intelligent addition to our written notes?  I chose Tapook the Magnificent, partly because he was always available round the camp; partly because the ponderous deliberations of his mind took him beyond the range of intellect of the average Dafla.  For instance, an ingenious but easily understood piece of our equipment such as a pair of scissors was not accepted as another miracle by Tapook, as it was accepted by the rest of the Daflas. Tapook would take up the scissors, examine them carefully, test them, and then peer at them intently for a full half-hour without speaking. Finally he would lay them down, grunt, and nod approval. If I followed his thought aright it was this: "Here I have a cunningly conceived but simple instrument. It is not beyond my own powers to invent such a thing, but I must confess that it would never have occurred to me. It may be deduced, however, that certain other more miraculous articles of theirs may well be explained by superior mental powers, and not necessarily by superhuman ones." Judging by his general attitude he may well have added the reservation: "It behoves me to be on my guard and not betray my ignorance, for should I do so I shall lose face with the men with whom I shall continue to live after these others are gone." On the present occasion I had no difficulty in persuading Tapook to leave his seat on the kitchen bench and join me at the central table. He gazed with some distrust at the sheets of foolscap, but appeared quite willing to be entertained. I began by drawing a portrait of Tapook himself with a few bold pencil strokes. This was a good beginning for Tapook recognised his likeness at once and smiled broadly for the first and last time I remember. I then drew the basha, Frank's tent and a passing mithan, all of which were highly commended. I did not assay an imaginary buru for I felt that if I did finally succeed in getting Tapook to put pencil to paper he would only produce a buru copied from my own.

At length I turned the paper round and gave Tapook the pencil. He clenched his teeth on his pipe and clamped his fist round it as if he quite expected it to hop out of his fingers and run away. Finally he made a minute mark in the centre of the page. This he followed with a few more, closely adjacent marks produced with such infinite labour that perspiration began to stand out on his forehead. At the end of half an hour he had used no more of the paper than might have been covered by a half-crown piece. At that, he flung the pencil away in disgust, began massaging his cramped fingers, and was lost to the drawing-board for ever. What he had tried to depict I have no idea; it looked like some character of Chinese hand-writing with a number of spelling mistakes!

The lesson did have one good effect. Tapook had failed in his first contest with natives of the world; but he was determined that his position as prince among the natives of the valley should remain unchallenged. Hitherto, he had been as useless about the camp as a chair with a broken leg; now, he lent a hand at any task which he considered worthy of his prowess. Thus when Tameng began plaiting a huge mat of split bamboo to act as canopy over our open fireplace, Tapook joined in with a will, working fully as deftly and swiftly as the Apa Tani. On another occasion Washington was splitting logs for the fire, and making hard work of it until Tapook unsheathed his dao and shattered the logs as if they had been so many match-sticks. A fine picture he made too, his splendid muscles tensed as he poised his huge two-handed sword high above his head before bringing it crashing down upon the wood.

I remember one other instance of his superior judgment. In the middle of our stream Pio Pio had placed a soap box as platform to assist him in drawing water. The top of the box was nearly flush with the surface of the stream. One day a Dafla youth standing beside our basha shot off an arrow at the box and missed it. This gave us an idea for another archery competition—a packet of cigarettes for anyone who could stick an arrow in the box. This time the range was a mere twenty yards, but it proved a difficult shot for the angle was so oblique that all arrows which struck the top of the box bounced off it and buried themselves in the far bank of the stream. Tapook considered this problem for some time. Then he spanned his great bow, and aimed deliberately a short distance in front of the box. His arrow glanced off the surface of the water and stuck unerringly in the inch or so of the side elevation which showed above the stream.

As far as drawing was concerned, there was only one other man in the valley who might possibly make a draughtsman: Nana, the priest. But apart from occasional flashes of amiability, Nana was a surly, suspicious man, the ringleader of the non-co-operative Daflas and obviously the prime mover in influencing Dodum against us. We could not even get Nana to swallow a paludrine pill, although he suffered badly from recurrent malaria.

For us, the most pleasurable hours of the day were those of the late afternoon and evening. The last watcher at the swamp would return at four-thirty and we would then sit down to a magnificent tea of buttered oatmeal cakes and raspberry jam. We all ate enormously which was not surprising, for regular exercise, air like wine, and long, deep sleep had brought the three of us to the peak of physical condition. At last came the evening when I could perform the great unveiling ceremony and emerge from the chrysalis of Elastoplast in which I was swathed. The two ends of the broken collar-bone had slipped slightly out of place which was not surprising but they were well-knit. If an insignificant deformity was to be the only price demanded from me for participating in the hunt for the buru, I was quite prepared to pay it. But for some time my left shoulder and arm remained pitifully weak and I continued to dread the succession of tight-rope acts across the pole bridges which had to be negotiated on the way to the Buru Swamp. However, once more I could wash and scrub myself, and how luxurious one felt when one emerged glowing from the leaf-screened bathroom with a clean shirt on one's back!

Our bathing routine over, we squatted round the new-lit camp fire, sipping our nightly tot of rum, or rice-spirit. This latter was a fiery, fearsome drink, but diluted with ginger-beer essence, or lemonade powder it did us no harm. The sun would set in a gory welter of monsoon clouds as we sat down to supper by the light of hurricane lamps. The meal over we would talk for an hour, the clearing around us spangled with countless dancing fire-flies. Both Charles and Frank had many tales to tell of the frontier tribes of Burma and Assam. Frank had even accompanied an expedition which had penetrated to the wild Wa headhunters of the Sino-Burma frontier. I had no contribution to make, but we were lucky in that we all had much the same interests and I, at least, was an untiring listener.

We usually turned in at eight-thirty, for by that time we were beginning to doze in our chairs. The first hour of the night was generally a disturbed one. In the kitchen hut we could hear Orenimo and Pio Pio still chuckling over their rice beer. Occasionally their two melodious voices would join harmoniously in singing some mission hymn, for which, we suspected, they had their own ribald words, for more often than not the hymn would break off in a gusty gale of laughter. Every now and then a mithan would duck under the fence ropes and renew the quest for salt. Then, there would be a snort and a great waft of milky breath would invade one's tent. But the tireless dog Kiro would be on his feet in a second and a plunging, snorting devil dance would begin round the camp, with Kiro barking furiously, half in anger, half in play, and the bewildered mithan, foiled in his search, lunging desperately for the weak spot in the fence where he had broken in upon us. If the task proved too much for Kiro one of us would have to turn out and chase off the intruder with a flaming brand from the camp fire.

Almost every night it rained. First, a gentle flurry on the roof of the tent, then a staccato tattoo like buck-shot dropping on a drum-head. More and more frequently we began to experience tremendous monsoon thunderstorms. When these occurred the very ground beneath the tents trembled and a deluge, which must have been of the order of inches an hour, pounded down upon the slender spans of silk.

But awe-inspiring though these moments were, they again provided us with a feeling of infinite luxury, for the silk held, and the ground-sheets, no more than six feet by four which each of us occupied, remained dry, and we upon them were comfortable and warm in our beds, while all about us was a lake of seething, gurgling water. Sometimes, at the height of the storm, lightning would strike one of the jungle giants near us. At once the whole tree would be enveloped in a pillar of white fire. If the blow were severe, and the fire caught, the tree would finally topple and crash to the accompaniment of snapping and cracking vines and creepers giving way under weight of the trunk like the stays of a falling mast. But no fire could live long under that downpour, and never did we have the slightest fear of a general forest conflagration.

# CHAPTER XIV

# A Mithan Sacrifice

WE HAD NOT BEEN LONG AT RILO BEFORE WE BECAME VAGUELY uneasy about the amount of rainfall. Looking back along our journey we could remember a succession of storms starting as early as our crossing of the Brahmaputra at Gauhati. At the times they had occurred, we had been inclined to dismiss them merely as exceptional and out of reason. But now they were rapidly increasing in frequency. Two things were apparently necessary to ensure the appearance of the buru, adequate rain, and midsummer temperatures. Now, we had mid-April temperatures with June rainfall. If the same conditions continued, in June the temperature would be correct, but we might well have August rain conditions, in which case we could abandon all hope of getting back to Lokra until September. We were not, as yet, gravely concerned, for we were reluctant to believe that the monsoon had set in upon us in its full unrelenting force; we still hoped for a spell of clear, warm weather, to enable the sun to catch up with the rain. On dull rainy days, when there was no point at all in keeping watch at the swamp, Frank and I accompanied Charles down to the village. Nearly always some event of local importance was in progress. A village ceremony, attended with special rites, was the making of poisoned arrows. We arrived by accident on one occasion while this was going on and found we were far from welcome. We were allowed to watch the trimming and shaping of the shafts and the beating out of the metal arrow-heads upon flat stones. This all took place round the central table. The application of the actual poison was the concern of one particular brave who sat apart and forbade us to come near him. Photographs were out of the question. All we could see, from a distance, was that the poison resembled black putty, and was kneaded round the shaft next to the arrowhead, by the fingers, which were liberally moistened by the tongue in the process. While the chief operator sat scowling and licking his fingers, it was explained to us that should we approach him too closely, the "virtue" of the poison would be dissipated, leaving the arrowhead harmless. It looked an ugly business and we were not inclined to argue.

It was not long before we discovered that half our trouble in obtaining food lay in the fact that all live-stock had been reserved for particular barter transactions with neighbouring villages. In these exchanges, each animal and each article involved was not judged by its intrinsic value, but by the exterior circumstances which had played upon it during its existence. A mithan was never just *any* mithan; it was a particular beast, judged by past history, previous ownership, and so on. The same was the case with ornaments, necklaces and everything else that came up for exchange. One could never say: "two necklaces equal one pig"; for one particular necklace, of no more apparent value to us than a thousand others, might have some historical connection which made it worth twenty pigs.

When we were in Rilo the mountains round about had been virtually shot out for miles around; in fact one could walk for days without seeing a living thing. Inter-village visiting and trading, therefore, was rivalling hunting as the main amusement, and families would be setting off incessantly on excursions lasting some days, or in their turn receiving visits from relations who lived in more distant parts.

One morning we found the village in an unusual state of commotion. Carrying baskets were being stuffed with provisions; gourds filled with rice beer; head-bands for the baskets were being fashioned from strips of bark; two mithans had been rounded up and stood stamping impatiently, tethered by fibre halters to the centre table. Everyone was in the highest spirits and for once our presence was not resented. It transpired that a more than usually elaborate barter deal had been clinched which involved three villages. Rilo, whose party was now forming up, had mithan to spare and wanted cloth and a young bride for one of the braves. Vayjo, a day's march away, had two Thibetan bells and a bride to spare and wanted mithan. Gangate, two days' march away, had cloth and wanted bells. It had been arranged, heaven knows after how much argument and how much preliminary visiting, that Rilo should take two mithan to Vayjo in return for the Thibetan bells and the bride. Rilo would then pass on the bells to Gangate in return for cloth. Normally Dodum should have headed the party, but probably owing to our presence in the valley he had elected to remain behind and leadership had devolved on Tapook and the priest Nana. Both men were resplendent in their best clothes and ornaments. Tapook had produced an eagle's-wing fan for the occasion, and as the party moved off he led the procession chanting to the good spirits to bless the journey and waving his fan to ward off the evil ones.

Some four days later the party returned by way of our camp, chanting defiantly to the evil spirits as they came across our clearing. All the men appeared mightily pleased with themselves, as well they might, for the first part of the deal had been concluded to the satisfaction of both parties, and had led to an immense feast and much drinking of rice beer. After some persuasion Nana produced one of the bells, which he was carrying in a small cane basket. He probably reasoned that there could be no harm for Rilo in displaying it to us, for he was merely acting as its trustee until such time as it could be passed to Gangate. The bell was about six inches high and had no clapper. Its sole worth was vested in its history which consisted of a lengthy tour of all Daflas villages for many miles around. Its value as a curio in Delhi would be about three shillings.

The production of the bell, coupled with our well-feigned admiration and the general air of a bargain well-struck, put everyone in the best of spirits once more. Further supplies of rice-beer were brought from the village, we added the dregs of our toddy, and an uproarious morning was spent by all. But while there were bells for Gangate, there was no belle for Rilo, for she was considered too young, as yet, to leave her parents' house.

On another morning we arrived in the village to find a ceremony of a very different kind in progress. News had been received of an ailing mithan. This prospect of fresh meat pleased everyone except the unfortunate owners, who, however, had placed their faith in Nana. This gentleman sat crossed-legged on the centre-table intoning an interminable chant while beside him stood a basket full of young chickens. Every ten minutes, or so, the chant died, Nana reached in the basket, pulled out a squeaking chicken and cut its throat.

This performance Frank was permitted to film—probably because the greater part of the village was more interested in the death of the mithan than its survival—but I doubt if Frank's picture will ever be shown. Frank himself thought not: "Wonderful sequence that," he said between shots. "First time it's ever been taken, but we can't use it. Can't cut a chicken's throat in a cinema!"

The owners hoped that should a sufficient number of chickens be sacrificed the life of the mithan itself might be spared. This hope proved vain; three days later, after a large number of chickens had been done to death, Nana decreed that the mithan must be slaughtered. We had suspected that something of the sort might happen as the larders of the village had obviously been much depleted by the recent trading excursion and its attendant feasting. Thus, we were standing by to witness the sacrifice. This we were not permitted to do. It took place early one morning, without any warning being given to us. By the time we arrived in the village a large fire had been built beside the central table, the carcass had been dragged up to it, skinned and cut up on the spot. Cooking pots had already been produced, and a large portion of the mithan was in the process of being consumed. We, ourselves, came in for a small piece of steak, which although tough and stringy, proved very eatable after we had pounded it for some minutes and dressed it with onions.

While the fate of the mithan hung in the balance, an air of anxious suspense had settled over the village from a variety of motives. What had really taken place was an elaborate game of counting out, the person to be "it" depending on the whim of Nana's finger. Possibly the owners of the mithan had hoped to escape once more from the expense of providing meat for the whole village, although it must have been obvious that the die was heavily loaded against them. However, they could take their loss philosophically, for owing to the system of sacrificing roughly in turn, they would be able to dine free from other people's meat for many months to come.

We had much wanted to record the actual rites of sacrifice, which we believe have never been witnessed by Europeans, and were much depressed at having missed them, but by a great stroke of good fortune, Charles was able to fill in the details after our return to Lokra. Frank and I had already left for Calcutta and Charles was ready packed waiting to move off from Shillong, when he received news that a mithan was about to be sacrificed in a neighbouring Dafla village. He has sent me the following notes:

"Mithan are mainly sacrificed in order to propitiate evil spirits which have brought sickness to a household. When sacrificed a number of strange wooden carvings, looking like fretwork are put up on bamboo poles, and are enclosed in a kind of panel. These are little understood, but seem to be symbols of the more important spirits responsible for sickness. Very important among them is the sun. Alongside are put up other little structures of bamboo, in honour of lesser spirits. The ritual of the sacrifice differs within the tribe. A sacrifice I witnessed near Lokra was carried out by a headman who had recently recovered from a perforated gastric ulcer, and was more or less the fulfilment of a promise made to the spirits that he would sacrifice if he recovered.

"A young bull mithan was purchased—for 200 rupees—and the village concerned having no senior priest, one was engaged from a neighbouring village.

"Omens were taken as to the day. For two or three days before, the men of the household were engaged in making the wooden symbols, and painting rough designs on them. They were put up on the day of the sacrifice.

"Before the appointed day, the mithan was tethered to a post a few yards from the house. The proceedings began by the priest going round with a minor priest in attendance as an acolyte, and carrying a flasked-shaped gourd, while the priest carried a large mop, made of frayed-out bamboo.

"He went round and round the builders of the panel, chanting low and monotonously, occasionally waving his mop, and apparently uttering some sort of blessing. The same was done to the mithan. The building of the panel took the whole morning, the builders being served with beer at reasonable intervals. Once some women came out and spread rice paste on the horns of the mithan, and on the panel. When the construction was completed, all the men went inside the long house of the headman. He, himself, was in festive dress, and wore great tubular ear-rings of silver, and a broad band of silver round his head, surmounted in front by a bow-shaped silver ornament.

"Inside the house all men and boys (not women) started a slow and rather monotonous chant, and danced a series of shuffling dances, round and round inside. This was to the time of a flat, plate-like gong, an heirloom probably centuries old. The priest also went inside and wandered round blessing the house and the dancers.

"After an hour or so of this, everyone came out, carrying many chickens, a small pig and a small goat, which they quickly hung up on the sacrificial posts. The mithan was tethered to the front of the panel. Two arrows were taken by the priest, who held them towards the mithan and commenced a long incantation. They were then shot into it from close range by a young man of the family. Immediately afterwards it was quickly and humanely dispatched by another man with a small axe. The pig, goats and fowls were also killed as quickly as possible. The liver was taken out of both mithan and pig for reading (from its shape) omens as to whether the sacrifice was successful. The meat was then divided, and a leg given as a fee to the senior priest."

To this account I feel it only fair to add that, the village involved being on the edge of the plains, the traditional ceremony had probably been subject to outside influences, and was more elaborate than could have been expected of Daflas of the interior. As I have already said, Rilo Daflas had no art, no music, no dancing, and no means of recording anything except orally from one generation to another.

Following the death of the Rilo Mithan, a device was erected next to the table, consisting of two stakes, the one forked and the other straight, and in line with each other. The second stake bore a piece of the mithan's hide still bearing the hair. It occurred to me, rather fancifully I fear, that the device was the simplest form of symbolism meant to represent that the mithan was still alive, and thus to appease passing spirits who might be offended by its death. Charles, however, recognised the device at once as a common fertility symbol, the forked stake being female and the straight stake male.

CHAPTER XV

# Pingling and Pinchio

FOR SOME WEEKS THE ROUTINE AT THE SWAMP WAS unvaried. Tameng and Taning between them had made the observation post as comfortable as we could wish for. They had made a hollow in the hill-side, and constructed a long low bench, with a canopy overhead to shield us from the sun and rain. In front of the bench they erected a stand to hold the telescope, while behind they made another rough platform for themselves.

Watch-keeping was a restless, uncomfortable business for dim-dams and all manner of other insects were far more plentiful at the swamp than in the camp. However, the jungle round the clearing gradually became oppressive to us, and it was good to be out in the free air with an unobstructed view over a wide stretch of country.

For some time I used to ponder what we might do to prompt the buru to make an early appearance, but I regret that I could think of nothing. The whole of the swamp lay before us like an arena, all that was lacking were the performing animals. It is true that a small inlet of the swamp in the north-east corner was hidden from us by a projection of Lookout Hill, but it seemed highly unlikely it could hide anything.

One morning I took time off and explored this corner with Tameng. We followed the jungle path along the top of Lookout Hill going on past the point where Frank and I had previously turned off down towards the swamp. In due course we came out on another derelict "jhoom", or clearing, at the apex of the angle where the hill joined the northern mountain barrier. The hidden inlet was now exposed to us, but a single glance showed me that the reeds covering the floor there, were as unbroken as anywhere else and that, therefore, further investigation was useless. Seen from this new point, more of the two central pools was visible, than from the observation post. In addition, two or three small secondary pools were apparent, as well as a stretch of the tributary stream which penetrated the swamp, but in my estimation the improvement in the view was scarcely sufficient to justify us moving the observation post, entailing as that would, at least an extra hour's walking each day.

On the way back through the jungle I was suddenly startled by the piercing, hysterical shrieks of a brain-fever bird, so close that at first I thought the bird must be about to perch on my shoulder. This proved to be Tameng's particular way of amusing himself. The chirrupings and pipings of his bird imitations were so perfect that soon answering calls would be coming back to him from all parts of the jungle. At all times it was an education to watch him moving with his lithe, stealthy step through the jungle. His eyes would be shifting constantly this way and that, as he sought for something that might be of service to us. On this occasion he pointed out a slender sapling with his dao, cut it down with a couple of strokes and began collecting the fruit which looked like clusters of green elder-berries. They had a strong citron flavour and they made excellent natural lemonade.

It is now high time for me to introduce two charming characters with the authentic Walt Disney names of Pingling and Pinchio. It would hardly seem possible to find a people more simple than the Daflas, but at Rilo we discovered the remnants of a tribe known as Sulungs, who were looked down upon, even by the Daflas, as "jungly persons".

The Sulungs are of different origin from the Daflas, and the two languages are not mutually understandable. The Sulungs were probably in the Dafla Hills before the Daflas arrived from the East.

9

In a few parts they have their own, independent villages, but over most of the area they are entirely subservient to the Daflas. The relationship is an interesting one, and many Dafla villages have a small Sulung settlement attached, and dependent on them. The advantages to the Daflas are: (i) Help in their fields; (ii) help for house building and other ordinary activities; (iii) help in porters for their eternal trading parties; (iv) help for hunting and food gathering in times of scarcity.

On their side the Sulungs are given: (i) freedom to cultivate and hunt over the lands which belong, nominally at least, to the Daflas: (ii) protection from attack by raiders; (iii) the loan of such rough implements as the Daflas may possess.

In Rilo, the Sulung settlement was fifteen minutes' climb up the mountainside from the Dafla village. It consisted of two huts only, perched on a spur like Alpine chalets. In these lived Pinchio and his wife and son, and Pingling, whose wife had just died, with his mother and small daughter. There is no inter-marriage between Sulung and Dafla, and Pingling was now negotiating for a second wife with a Sulung settlement many days' journey away.

In dress, in the shape of their houses and in many of their habits, the Sulungs closely copy the Daflas, but there can be no argument that they are of different and very possibly superior stock. Pinchio was shy and seldom removed his hand from in front of his face when talked to, but Pingling was as merry as a cricket and quite as intelligent as any Rilo Dafla. Pingling claimed that he came from a village three weeks' journey away "under the snows", by which he meant the Himalayas.

Both he and Pinchio were tireless workers—the habitual sloth of the Dafla men was unknown to them—and between them they had cleared a huge area of mountainside jungle, first by felling the giant trees with their daos, and then by firing the undergrowth. The sowing of rice and maize was then left to the women-folk, while the men turned to some other task.

We spent some time with the Sulungs for, to the best of our knowledge, no European had ever yet been able to make a complete record of them. By the time we had finished our work Frank had succeeded in shooting a fine film in colour giving the story of "A day in the life of Pingling and Pinchio".

Pingling, unlike the Daflas, proved a ready actor in front of the camera; in fact, for Frank, he became as good as an assistant director, for he was constantly interpolating various deft little touches of his own. Pingling felling a tree, Pingling shooting an arrow or Pingling bouncing his baby on his back, were all good sequences; but Pingling stalking an imaginary pig was a masterpiece of pantomime which made us all rock with laughter.

Between crops, the Sulungs live largely on jungle plants, and one day Pingling led us into the forest and pointed out a sizeable tree fern. This he felled and trimmed, finally cutting sections from the white "meat" of the stem. This "meat" he pulped with an improvised mallet on a stone held between his toes. He then buried the pulp under leaves in order to soften the fibre. Two or three days later he retrieved the pulp which he gave to Pinchio's wife Narbe, who squeezed out surplus moisture by kneading it in a rush basket. She then prepared for us a spongy flap-jack which after toasting, had very much the taste and consistency of crêpe rubber!

The chief living of the Sulungs, and this held good for our own little settlement, is got by hunting, at which they are probably unexcelled throughout India. Men like Pingling and Pinchio are as much a part of the jungle as the animals they follow. Often they will disappear for weeks at a time with their entire families, carrying their babies on their backs and sleeping wherever the chase takes them. We were, in fact, most lucky to have caught them "at home" for, for the better part of the year, their two little chalets lie completely deserted except for a scratching cockerel or two.

One day, when the film was still incomplete, the Daflas brought word to us that Pingling and Pinchio were off on another excursion. They had left without warning, forgetting another meeting we had arranged for the following day, and we never saw them again.

To fill in a few more details of their strange life I again quote from Charles's notebook: "Their position is really that of feudal retainers. Nominally they are at the beck and call of the Daflas, but actually they live their own lives quite freely, and the relationship is a perfectly amicable one in spite of the swaggering and boasting of the Daflas as to their overlordship. If they were to be 'freed' from the Daflas, the Sulungs would soon be crowded out and go under altogether, and it is probably due entirely to this pact of mutual convenience that they owe their survival at all. They are far freer than industrial labour under big business. They are usually attached to a leading clan of a Dafla village, and if the clan moves the Sulungs go as well.

"They practise very simple cultivation round their little villages, which are of two or three houses at the most, and joined on to, or near the Dafla village they are attached to.

"Crops are rice, and maize. Their rice keeps them going for several months, and for the rest of the year they go out on long food-gathering expeditions, for up to two or three or more months at a time, into the jungle; everyone, men, women and children, deserting the village.

"Details of organisation of these parties are not known, but it is known that they subsist mainly on wild sago, from a small sago palm, and made also from the pith of a tree-fern. The palm is preferred, as the fern pith takes some days to macerate out the fibre. Sago takes only a day or less to prepare from the palm, and is made by a series of washings and strainings of the pith.

"For hunting, the village party seems to split up into ones

and twos. All hunting is done with bow and arrow: the poison used comes from a root and is traded in from more distant areas to the north.

"They are occasionally polygamous, but as a rule can afford only one wife. The normal price is a mithan and a cloth.

"The Sulungs are very skilful, and make expert blacksmiths and weavers, etc. It is probable that they learnt these arts from other tribes.

"Their religion is quite unstudied, but is almost certainly of the very simplest—jungle spirits, hunting spirits, water spirits, and so on. Most of their present religious customs are said to be borrowed from the Daflas. They are in no sense a degenerate people. In spite of their very simple way of life, they have nothing in common as regards appearance with people like the Andaman Islanders, or Malay 'Primitives'."

So much for Charles's notes; but what better description could there be of the life of merry Pingling and shy Pinchio, than these lines of Addison?

> "Coarse are his meals, the fortune of the chace,
>   Amid the running streams he slakes his thirst,
>   Toils all the day and at the approach of night,
>   On the first friendly bank he lays him down,
>   Or rests his head upon a rock till morn,
>   And if the following day he chance to find
>   A new repast or an untasted spring,
>   Blesses his stars and thinks it luxury."

# CHAPTER XVI

# The Next Blow

MAY CAME, AND THERE COULD NO LONGER BE ANY DOUBT about it; heavy rainfall had continued throughout April; it was too late to expect any respite before the setting in of the monsoon. We had had the misfortune to strike an utterly abnormal year. Climatically, we were at least a month ahead of the calendar date. In the few clear intervals the sun shone strongly. Conditions for the buru were ideal; but the weeks had slipped by with none of us able to report a single significant sign of life in the swamp.

The water-level had risen appreciably; about five pools were now visible from the observation post, but they were still very far from joining and creating an expanse of open water. We now had serious doubts if they ever would.

Under the alternate impetus of rain and sun the vines creepers and matted, fleshy jungle plants appeared to be growing with almost malignant urgency. The path through the valley floor was a morass. The tiny flowers there were inundated; the wild raspberries had ripened and were now sodden and tasteless. The vein-like, crystal clear, cheerful little streams were roaring with tumbling brown water. The mountainsides round the valley smoked with low-hanging cottonwool clouds. Everything one touched was damp and sticky with monsoon moisture. Our blankets "sweated"; the tents and the hut teemed with dim-dams, sand-flies, thumb-nail-size jungle ticks and other insects. Lizards scampered about the camp; at night frogs croaked about our feet and sometimes leapt from the floor of the hut to our shoulders in one hop.

Daflas, returning from hunting trips, came through the

camp with their legs streaming blood from leech bites. Behind us, towards the plains, the Pakke River was reported temporarily unfordable.

We slopped round the camp in damp boots and wet and dirty clothes. It was useless to wash anything; there was nowhere to dry it. The damp got into Frank's cameras and a good deal of film was lost until we hit on the plan of storing them over the kitchen stove. The only thing in the camp that flourished to our infinite pleasure was the Pakke orchid, which suddenly emerged as a glorious fragile, fleece of thirty-three blossoms.

Watch-keeping had become a spasmodic affair, for there was no point in sitting out in the pouring rain, but whenever the clouds showed any sign of clearing we were back, once more, in the old position. Surely, we felt, if the buru is to appear, it must be now or never.

I remember the day the next blow fell because of an odd incident which immediately preceded it. Charles had had the afternoon watch of the day before; I, the next forenoon. It was a steamy, drowsy morning. The heavy rain of the night had passed, the sky was a misty blue but down in the south the clouds were already banking up again. For some time I sat brooding, chin in hand, staring out over the empty swamp, with Tameng snoring gently on the platform behind me. I was pondering the strange life of Pingling and Pinchio when suddenly I caught a low drumming note in the air. The noise grew louder and I noticed that it was emitted by a truly enormous hornet, its body about three inches long and barred with black and amber bands. It was a veritable Superfortress of an insect and with some alarm I watched it suddenly change flight and wheel towards me. I sat frozen while its wing-beats ruffled the hair at the nape of my neck, then it sheered away, turned once more and made for Tameng. The Apa Tani heard it coming in his sleep, and in one fantastic movement he had bounded up like an un-leashed spring, drawn his dao and smashed the unfortunate insect out of the air with the edge of the blade. It was an incredible exhibition of instantaneous reflex action, coming as it did out of deep slumber. For one second poor Tameng sat glaring at me with bleary eyes, as if I had been the cause of the intrusion. Then he shook his head, grinned cheerfully and settled down once more on his couch. The hornet lay shattered with shivered wings in the grass, waiting until the red ants could make a meal of it.

Half an hour after this episode Charles appeared. Looking grave, he sat down beside me and then announced: "I fear we are in for a great disillusionment." At this point I can feel my readers saying: "Aha! so he intends to bamboozle us after all. He has sought an elaborate excuse to tear us away from our homes, lead us up into wild, comfortless country. Now he intends to desert us, empty-handed, in a desolate swamp." But may I remind you that we were not just three romantics; we were a soldier, a journalist and a scientist, all hard-bitten, and of the three of us the most sceptical all along had been the scientist, ever searching for some argument to disprove his own evidence, yet carried onwards in spite of himself. We believed, because the weight of the evidence left so little room for doubt. Nor have we yet finished with the buru, not by any means.

However, what Charles had to relate was this: that morning he had gone down to the village, and had met a hunting party who announced firmly that they had seen the buru in the swamp in the middle of the previous afternoon. Charles had then recollected that at about the same time he had seen some puzzling shadows on the surface of one of the pools with the naked eye, but with the telescope had proved them to be nothing more than wind rippling the surface. He said, possibly too precipitately: "What you mean is that what you saw in the pool were shadows on the surface."

At this, the Daflas had wagged their heads and grunted as much as to say: "Well, if that's all you think the buru is, you may well be right." This was such a staggering change of front that Charles had toiled up Lookout Hill in order to summon me to another council of war. A very gloomy session it was. We began by deciding that we needed some solace and encouragement, and Frank had gone in search of our one remaining bottle of rum. This could not be found, and finally we wrote it off as having been among the stores looted by the Lokra porters.

Charles was at first completely prepared to accept this new Dafla opinion and was very depressed. Frank and I, having had no part in the conversation, were downcast, but inclined to argument. To my mind the detailed description of the buru and its habits given so frequently and unvaryingly by so many Daflas could not be easily dismissed. It seemed unbelievable that successive generations of men who depend for their livelihood on hunting, which in its turn depends on the keen observation of wild animals, could all have been deceived into making an animal out of a shadow on the surface of a pool. Even if we were to concede this, a host of other questions remained unanswered. The whole countryside had been positive that burus appeared only at Rilo. If the buru was merely a shadow, why should it not also inhabit the equally large swamps at Chemgung and Pakke?

What was the link between the Rilo burus and those of the Apa Tani valley, fifty miles distant over a succession of ranges, where lived another tribe speaking another language? No paths led East to the Apa Tanis; the country was reported to be very difficult indeed. The burus of the Apa Tanis were known to have been extinct for centuries. Why should the same animal, bearing the same name, suddenly reappear at Rilo, which had only been inhabited a mere ten years? These questions and many others were beyond us. We all agreed that we were ill-served by our interpreters. Padme was too young and diffident to carry much weight with seasoned warriors. Taning the irrepressible, was aggressively flamboyant with them, and too inclined to make fun of such men as Dodum and Nana as "savages". They, in their turn, resented being laughed at; we thought it quite possible that they were embarrassed by our failure to see the buru after they had sworn to its presence and had fallen in with Charles's suggestion merely to save face. It was obvious, too, that they would seize at any chance to be rid of us, and they might well think that at long last they had hit upon the best method of encouraging us to leave.

We decided to wait for the appearance of Jum Jar, the head government interpreter, who had been reported to us as being on a bride-seeking expedition which would bring him past the camp in a few days' time on his way home.

Nevertheless, a good deal of enthusiasm for the hunt had gone out of us. Now that we could no longer rely on the Daflas, now that a strong element of doubt had entered into things, we were forced to admit that the swamp looked a dreary, unlikely place to harbour any sort of animal.

Jum Jar's search for a bride proved a lengthier business than we had anticipated. A further ten days of heavy rain passed before he was reported at Chemgung, a morning's march away. During this time we snatched at the brief sunny intervals to complete our record of both still and moving pictures.

Neither Tapook, nor Nana would face the camera; they held to the belief that much of a man's "virtue" departs from him when his likeness is reproduced on paper. They had obviously worked this out from the pictures we had shown them, and they dreaded the thought that a reproduction of themselves should go with us which we could curse or torture at our pleasure. Frank spent much of his time dodging about behind the huts trying to "capture" Tapook with a telescopic lens, but only twice did he succeed. Dodum submitted to the scrutiny of the "evil eye", but only under protest. No doubt he felt that having balked us in many things he could no longer afford to be unco-operative and that his position as Government-appointed headman might be at stake if Jum Jar got to hear of his previous conduct. Tapook's little boy Ria and Dodum's young son Senyak reflected the attitude of their fathers. Senyak would pose unconcernedly; I spent hours trying to distract Ria's attention with my wrist-watch, with simple conjuring tricks, and with my typewriter, but always he would keep a wary eye open for Frank, and would squirm away or duck under the table as soon as the camera appeared. Ria had an elusive, impish grin which we knew would make a particularly attractive picture; but apart from that we wanted his photograph to complete our record of hair styles. Under tens, like Ria, had their heads completely shaved except for a long-forelock. Over tens but under sixteens, like Senyak, wore their hair long, braided by a cane headband threaded with metal studs. Over sixteens adopted the adult style of a cane skull-cap and a bun bound over the forehead. Young girls had their heads cropped, possibly, as with the Naga tribes, as a sign of virginity. Upon marriage they were permitted to grow their hair long.

The day of Jum Jar's arrival was memorable for a number of reasons. Firstly, the sun came out clear and strong after another night of tremendous rainfall which had again brought our pleasant brook to a condition of high spate. Then, in the course of the morning another four Gurkha runners arrived from the plains bringing mail bags sent up to us by Noble and Menzies. This time the runners had been delayed three days on the banks of the Pakke before they could make the crossing. They had finally struggled across in water almost up to their necks. Their provisions were spoiled or exhausted and generally they were in pretty poor shape. The bright sunshine had brought a more than usually large party of Daflas back to the camp. Prominent among them were Tapook and Ria, the lad Senyak and many other children, all of whom at once began the old game of cadging cigarettes for the Tapook pouch. Everyone was in good spirits. There was much joking, some bewildered fooling with my typewriter, some desultory archery, and then, on a sudden, a tumultuous outcry from the servants' hut.

This hut was open on the side facing the brook and stood only about two yards from the edge of the bank whence a six-foot ladder led down into the water. The whole of the side of the bank was covered with a dense mat of undergrowth against which the ladder lay. Orenimo, Pio Pio, two of the Gurkhas and a handful of Daflas were standing at the top of the ladder when suddenly a huge snake was sighted a few feet below them. This snake was described as ten feet long, thicker than a man's arm and of a deadly poisonous variety. This description was sufficient to bring Charles, usually blasé about all serpents, running from the hut, for a poisonous snake of that length could very possibly be the much feared Hamadryad, or King Cobra.

The hunt was on in a trice; daos and kukris flashed and ten or a dozen Daflas, bare-footed and bare-legged, jumped down the bank into the undergrowth and were soon slashing away, half in the water and half out. At the top of the bank, directing operations with his huge dao, stood the imperturbable Tapook, beside him Frank with his camera, Charles and myself. But although an immense noise was made, and an occasional glimpse of the snake seen, it finally escaped, no doubt by taking to the water and swimming downstream.

This snake was probably washed down upon us during the night, and we were heartily glad to see the last of it. Few snakes can be more terrible to face than the King Cobra, which, on occasion, will attack a human being unprovoked. This is especially true of the female with young.

King Cobras of eighteen feet in length have been recorded, and it is a known fact that when attacked, or attacking, they are capable of raising fully a third of their length off the ground. Their bite is probably the most deadly of all snakes owing to the amount of venom they can inject into a wound. No Dafla would ever tackle a King Cobra single-handed, but there is reasonable safety in numbers, for whichever way it turns a snake can only face one assailant at a time, and its entire length is then exposed to numerous other blows which it cannot see coming.

The hunt for the Hamadryad, with its foot by foot inspection of the undergrowth covering the bank of the stream, did, at least, turn up one interesting specimen—an eighteen-inch long, emerald-green, bamboo viper. For want of anything better we bore this into camp where Frank filmed it in colour and took a number of stills. I am sorry to say that this creature, which could have inflicted a dangerous bite on its own ground, came to a miserable end on ours. First it was barked at by Kiro, then pecked at by Orenimo's pet cockerel, then nearly trodden on by mistake by Taning, who came bouncing in a hurry out of the kitchen, and was given the fright of his life. Finally, it was decapitated by Tapook, with a ponderous dao stroke and flung into the stream by Charles. After a King Cobra, a bamboo viper was small fry, but Frank Noble later told me that it was from this species that he had his narrowest snake escape. He has planted the garden of his bungalow at Lokra with rare orchids gathered on his many treks. He was approaching one of the scented variety, which he had draped on a tree at face height, to smell it, when he suddenly saw a bamboo viper peering at him from among the blossoms. It was perfectly camouflaged and only about six inches away from his nose when he spotted it.

After the snakes, a monkey or squirrel, we never knew which. It was the only wild animal we ever saw on the expedition, and it appeared late in the morning jumping from tree to tree round the clearing. This was a chance for the bow and arrow men and for Frank and his rifle, but although it led us some distance into the jungle we finally lost it, and merely picked up a number of leeches for our pains.

Late in the afternoon Jum Jar arrived, with the obsequi-
ous Tagora dancing attendance. Jum Jar was a middle-aged
man of pleasant bearing and obviously of far greater
intelligence than our own interpreters.

He wore a scarlet sash and large brass badge of office,
both presented to him by the Government. Throughout the
Dafla country he was respected and regarded as a man of
authority. On his reports to Menzies rested the fate of many
a headman and well they knew it. In him our last hope of
getting to the bottom of the buru mystery rested.

That night round the fire Jum Jar listened gravely as we
"briefed" him about the buru. Occasionally he kicked the
garrulous Tagora, who sat cross-legged, sipping at a large
stoop of rice-beer, and interpolating an irrelevant remark
whenever he could find occasion to do so.

It was decided that Jum Jar should spend the night down
in the village in Dodum's house, and that we should visit
him in the morning to learn what he had been able to
discover.

# CHAPTER XVII

# Into the Swamp Again

THE NEXT MORNING ANOTHER LUDICROUS STROKE OF BAD
luck overtook us. We went early down to the village, only
to find Dodum's long house in an uproar. During the night
his senior wife had been taken ill with stomach ache. The
priest had been sent for, and Nana now sat on the porch,
where we had often paused to drink rice-beer, intoning his
endless chant for the sick, and taking the omens as to
whether a pig should be sacrificed or not. Taking the omens
in this case amounted to examining the yokes of hard-boiled
eggs to find if they were clear or blemished. A clear yoke
indicated a sacrifice. By the time we arrived about six eggs
had been halved at intervals of about an hour's chanting
each. All had been blemished, but the rite was still continu-
ing, and it was becoming increasingly apparent that Nana's
larder must again be empty. Dodum stood disconsolately
by, weighing up the respective disasters of losing a pig or a
wife. Jum Jar was impatiently kicking his heels.

The whole household had little time to spare for the buru
that morning, and Jum Jar had no easy time of it. In the
end, after a number of leading questions, and much unsatisfactory prompting, Jum Jar pronounced it as his opinion
that none present had actually seen the buru that year, and
possibly not in the past, but that everyone took it for granted
that it existed in the swamp. This was cold comfort and
confirmed us in our fear that the Daflas of Rilo were spoilt
for further questioning. Interrogation being over for the
morning, Frank Charles and I filled in an hour or so chasing
a domestic pig into the jungle, while Dafla archers shot
arrows as near to it as possible without hitting it. This was

as near as we could get to the climax of a hunt after wild pig
—a sequence which Frank required for his film.

The pig, a vicious old boar, showed no fear, could not be
stampeded into flight as the script demanded and, in fact,
frequently threatened to turn the tables by charging us.
We had some difficulty in restraining the archers from
shooting arrows into the animal's hams, and the exhibition
pleased everyone except the owner who finally had considerable trouble in persuading the pig to return to normal
civilised life.

Rain again fell heavily that afternoon and throughout the
night. On the following day Jum Jar called in on his way
back to Lokra—he was already long overdue there, and
could not afford to waste any more time with us. His visit
had been of little use except to heighten our suspicions that
there was no longer much point in prolonging the buru
hunt. Once more we called a council of war.

The whole case for the buru rested on the unanimity
with which all the Rilo Daflas had originally testified to its
existence. We had now shaken them from this stand; but
was the change of front genuine, or was it merely due to the
fact that they had found the weak chink in our armour; that
the best way to be rid of us was to deny the monster existed?
Frank and I, at least, thought that the Daflas' first story was
more likely to be the correct one; but there could be no doubt
about it that they were ruined as far as getting any more useful information was concerned. Was there anything we
could still do by ourselves? Whatever we decided would
have to be quickly executed. The monsoon was well upon
us. We were suffering no particular hardships; the worst
we had to endure was the incessant "ordeal by insect". But
there were other considerations. We had brought with us
food for 100 days. This had been depleted below the estimated ration by thefts on the trek up to the valley, and by
extra presents which we had been forced to give the Daflas
and Sulungs. We could still hold on until well into June.

But by that time the road back to Lokra would be utterly impassable. In the valleys the undergrowth would be so dense that we should have to hack our way yard by yard. No porter would be able to gain as much as a toe-hold on the greasy, endless paths threading their way up to the heights. The rivers which we had crossed at knee depth, would be at least up to our chests, bowling bone-crushing boulders down their beds; they would be unfordable, unbridgeable. The jungle paths would be seething with leeches. Should we delay too long, we ourselves might force the passage, but it would be at the cost of leaving all our equipment behind, for there would be no hope of getting any Dafla porter to accompany us. Either we must leave soon, or face the prospect of being marooned in Rilo, on starvation rations, until September when the rains ceased. Marooned with the buru was a tolerable prospect; without it, would be a senseless waste of time and money.

At length we agreed that the time had come to force the pace, and the best way we could think of doing so, was to make a last desperate effort to reach the two main central pools of the swamp. If that visit proved unproductive, the only alternative was to pack up and go home. None of us liked the prospect. So much water had fallen since our last excursion that the swamp was likely to be infinitely more treacherous. For a few minutes we considered the old plan of using one of the rubber boats to paddle down the stream and up the swamp tributary. We gave up the idea for the initial uncertainties remained, and we now had to add to them the possibility of meeting a Hamadryad at close quarters with not so much as a shot-gun to protect us. We decided that we should make our attempt along the old route, carrying two bamboo ladders with us so that we might progress by leap-frogging the one over the other if other means failed.

The first esential was to wait for at least two fine days in order to allow the water in the swamp to sink to a reasonable level. Fortunately, no sooner had we made up our minds to tackle the swamp again, when the rain held off and three days later we were able to make an early start. With us went Tameng, Taning and Padme.

We reached the top of Lookout Hill in good order, but so dense had the vegetation grown in the meantime, that we were lost the moment we turned off down the track which Frank and I had followed on our first sally. It was an appalling descent. Hemmed in on all sides by close-growing bamboo stems and tangled creepers, slipping, sliding and sometimes falling headlong, we went down what, in parts, amounted to a vertical cliff-face. When the slope eased off, as it occasionally did, there was the added danger of being impaled on bamboo spikes where stems had been cut a few inches above ground. These spikes were razor sharp, and steel-tough and would have inflicted a shocking wound had one fallen upon them.

However, an hour's back-breaking work saw us all safely assembled at the notched tree which marked our original jumping-off point at the swamp's edge. Here, while we stood around in the jungle twilight of high-noon, calf-deep in bubbling mire, picking leeches off each other's legs, and with a fortune in rare orchids hanging in delicately tinted sheafs about us, we waited while the two Daflas and Tameng cut and constructed the two bamboo ladders. Padme, who was right out of his element, soon cut a gash in his foot, and the bulk of the work fell, as it always seemed to do, on Tameng. But Tameng rose splendidly to the occasion, and very quickly he had two very serviceable ladders ready.

This time there was no pause for lunch; all of us realised that we had an unpleasant job ahead, and the sooner we had it behind us the better all of us would be pleased.

With the Daflas again hanging back, Charles and I picked up the first ladder and manhandled it through the first broad band of reeds and grass along the path we had originally cut.

The water here was appreciably higher than on our first trip, and the weight of the ladder caused us to sink deeper than formerly, but we got through the fringe without mishap, and once more stood at the edge of the belt of brown sedge. Behind us plodded Tameng shouldering the second ladder himself, then Frank with his various cameras.

The next step looked frightening, for so much rain had fallen that there appeared to be no buoyancy at all in the carpet of vegetation covering the swamp. For a few minutes we tried the leap-frog ladder method, but so heavy were the ladders that we soon exhausted ourselves without having made any discernible progress towards the pools. At that, after a brief spell of hesitation, we took our courage in both hands, put the ladders on our shoulders once more, and set off on a mad, floundering bee-line towards the pools. We argued that if one of us broke through the carpet, the rest of us could haul him out so long as he retained a grasp on a ladder. Our intention was to make as much progress as possible until we fell in, and from that point to revert to leap-frogging.

It so happened that, by luck, we chose the only tolerably firm line to the pools, and although we went down above the knee at each step, we actually managed to heave ourselves forward to the edge of the first pool. Here, there was virtually nothing beneath us but mud and water, and we flung the ladders down and clambered on them.

At long last we had reached our objective—the two main pools—which for so long had appeared so tantalisingly close, yet so intangible, as seen through the telescope. But a depressing anti-climax it proved. True, the first pool was about twice as large, both in length and breadth, as we had judged it, but even then it was quite apparent it could not have concealed as much as an otter from the intense observation under which we had held it for so many weeks. In addition, probing with a bamboo pole, we found it little more than three feet deep, with a bottom of stiffish mud.

With that waned any little optimism we might still have had about seeing the buru that season. A thunderstorm which had been piling up over the mountains, unnoticed by us, then broke, drenching us with water from above. Abandoning the ladders where they were, we broke from the pools and sloshed back, helter-skelter the way we had come, in any sort of order. My last memory of the swamp is of Frank, determined to get as complete a record as possible, rapidly sinking up to the waist with Taning, fumbling with a camera for the first time, trying to take his picture!

We arrived back at the camp like so many drowned rats. We were utterly dispirited and all of us had been badly bitten by leeches in spite of our precautions. I had been wearing canvas gaiters under trousers, with army anklets binding my trouser ends to the tops of my boots. Hair-thin when hungry, the leeches had worked their way up between trouser and gaiter, and now formed a bloated garter on each leg just below the knee. For the first time, that afternoon I had the depressing experience of bleeding from a score of bites; bleeding which none of our remedies could stop for some hours. That night we opened our last bottle of brandy—the buru's bottle—stoically preserved through many drinkless days for the occasion of his first undeniable appearance.

# CHAPTER XVIII

# Retreat

WE NOW CONSIDERED THAT WE HAD GIVEN THE BURU tradition as decent a burial as possible. The mystery remained. Our verdict, after much thought, was that there is no longer a buru at Rilo, but that one probably existed there until quite recent times, that is to say, until long after the burus of the Apa Tani tradition had been killed off. The burus of Rilo, in fact, may have existed until the time when the Daflas first began cultivating the jungle-covered sides of the swamp—say ten years ago. Once the surrounding mountainsides had been cleared of water-holding trees, the process of silting up within the swamp itself would be vastly accelerated, and this may have denied the buru any possibility of further existence. Having once seen the buru in the swamp, present-day Daflas may take its existence for granted; may even be deceived into thinking it is still there by deceptive shadows thrown by wind and clouds across the central pools. This is an unsatisfactory theory, but the best we could think of towards an explanation.

There was nothing left for us to do but to pack up and head back to Lokra. We now realised that we had made a mistake in trying to take a short cut to the monster. We should have done better to have begun with the bones in the Apa Tani valley; but it was now far too late in the season to make a fresh start.

The country to the east, the fifty miles which separated the Rilo Daflas from the Apa Tanis, looked tantalising. This area was left white for "unexplored" on our maps; it was strange to view those mountains from the top of Lookout Hill, and think that no white man had ever yet set foot among them. Possibly there lay another buru swamp; even a whole chain of buru swamps which would provide the link between the two valleys. But we no longer had the resources for a prolonged trek in unknown country in monsoon conditions, even if we could have found porters to accompany us. In any case, by committing ourselves to such an expedition, the hunt for the buru would lose all its concentration, and become a needle in a haystack affair which very probably would lead us nowhere. The main object of the search would be to establish whether any swamps exist between the Apa Tani valley and Rilo, and to begin interrogation once more from there. That was clearly a cold weather job.

Our immediate task was to get out of Rilo; and that was no easy matter. We needed sixty porters; the problem was where to get them. Tagora had remained with us and he was full of promises. He was well aware that there would be rich pickings for himself if he could get us back to Lokra. The next day he set off with his spry, bandy-legged, staff-supported gait, for Chemgung Village. He was back the same evening with the news that both Chemgung and Rilo flatly refused to help us. At that Charles's patience snapped. There was some excuse for Chemgung, but none at all for Rilo men who had benefited in countless ways from our visit. They had no other task on their hands; they spent their time lounging round the village drinking rice-beer.

Charles began by turning all Rilo Daflas out of the camp, forbidding them to come near us again. Even Tapook was included in the ban. He had been of no help at all in the buru hunt, and of little use about the camp, but he had become such a permanent fixture about the place that at length we had grown fond of him. Although we knew we were probably quite wrong, we had come to regard him as a friend and ally. But there could be no exceptions.

Then Tagora came in for a dressing down. The old man was horrified that he had fallen into disfavour. He was ordered to go out, scour the countryside far and wide, and be back within a week with sufficient men. He sprang to, with alacrity.

A cheerless week followed. A state of "cold war" existed between camp and village. Rain fell solidly with such force as we had never known. We became resigned to the possibility of being marooned in Rilo. On the fifth day word came through from Tagora that he had collected the porters, but that they were held up by a flooded marsh on the far side of Chemgung. They hoped to be in camp on the morrow, ready for an early start on the seventh day.

This was unexpectedly good news. We decided to send off an advance party to Lokra with a letter to Menzies asking for truck transport to come as far as it could to meet us. We chose two Gurkhas and Tameng. We thought it unwise to send less than three men. We needed the two remaining Gurkhas for our own party. Tameng went because he was the only person who could be regarded as a match for the Gurkhas, indeed he might even be an inspiration to them, but the camp felt strange without him.

We spent the next morning breaking camp and once more distributing the kit into forty-pound units. At noon the skies cleared, and the sun came out for the first time for days. Nothing could have pleased us better. That afternoon Charles, Frank and I paid a last visit to the swamp. The valley floor was now knee-deep in black mud. The main stream was a raging, roaring, vicious, scum-capped body of swirling coffee coloured water. The main bridge had been partially washed away and was on the point of collapsing altogether.

The swamp was its same old, blue-green, misty self. The two pools shone white and unruffled. No sailor has ever watched as intently for an enemy periscope as we had gazed at that tennis-court size patch of water in the hope of sighting a buru's snout. By now, wherever one's eyes roamed about the swamp instinctively they returned back to the pools. It was impossible for us not to feel a little foolish.

We spent some time in self-examination. Had we left anything undone which we might have done? We had never worked right round the mountains encircling the swamp; we had never probed down the rocky gorge where the stream left the valley. But we felt, rightly I am sure, that these schemes and others would merely have been elaborations of the initial task, and would have brought no positive contribution to it.

As we turned from the swamp for the last time all of us glanced back over our shoulders. It was an irresistible action; a billion to one chance that the last few seconds of our vigil would bring success. But it was not to be; for us the buru was dead.

No porters arrived in camp that night. We were not particularly anxious as the weather was definitely mending. We had allowed an extra day for the journey down in order to be sure that we should make our rendezvous with the truck transport. But it meant that from now on every march must be made to schedule.

Early on the next day Tagora arrived with his team. The old man was pleased with them as a hen with a brood of new chicks; but a sorry-looking bunch they were. They numbered a mere forty in all. In age they ranged from eight to eighty. Some were cripples, others were limping under the handicap of festering leg wounds. A good many were slaves from the remoter regions, quite obviously regarded as expendable by their headmen. Others were scalliwags who had brazenly joined the party in the hope of looting stores Only one man stood out; a tall, dignified elderly headman, named Thai, who was accredited to Government, and was therefore resplendent in a long scarlet cloak. Thai was going down to the plains to buy salt for his village. He was a welcome addition, for he looked ten times as reliable as Tagora.

Thai suffered from two afflictions, one of which I was later to discover in embarrassing circumstances. His immediate concern, however, was the fact that he was going bald, a rare complaint among primitive peoples. For Thai, loss of hair meant loss of face, and for that reason he covered his deficiency with a perky toque of black-cock feathers. Had we any cure for baldness? No, we had not, and poor Thai looked the picture of misery.

As for the remainder; Tagora went from one decrepit specimen to another, slapping him on the back and claiming that he was worth at least two Rilo Daflas. Nevertheless, it appeared laughable to imagine that the lot of them could possibly shift our bulky pile of baggage; particularly as we were still twenty men short.

Few of the new Daflas had ever had any contact with white men and they were as curious as kittens. They swarmed all over the camp, and as fast as we chased them out they swarmed back in again. It was not long before all manner of articles were missing, and the morning was punctuated by bursts of shouting and scuffling from the kitchen where a series of incursions was taking place.

In the middle of the confusion a "peace mission" arrived from Rilo headed by Nana carrying an offering of high-smelling mithan meat in a cane basket. After Nana, came Tapook with Ria and Dodum with Senyak. The attraction of visiting Daflas had proved irresistible; for Rilo there was also the possibility that there would be valuable parting gifts when we broke camp. Nana may even have argued that if Rilo were to escape a bad report it was high time that peace be made. But there were still to be no Rilo porters.

Tapook did not appear in the least offended at his suspension. When he saw Frank making a last desperate effort to photograph Ria, he actually seized the wriggling boy and forced him to pose. Possibly it had crossed his mind that the time had come to test the evil influence of the camera. Nothing would persuade Tapook to pose himself; but the fact that he had decided to risk his first-born son in the cause of science was a notable advance. We earnestly hoped that, for the future popularity of photography in Rilo valley, Ria did not subsequently go down with measles!

The lack of sufficient porters caused us to make another readjustment of the loads. We decided that we should leave the bulk of the rice for the porters' pay in the charge of Dodum, so that the men might collect it on their journey home. There was some risk that Dodum would try and keep it for himself after we had gone; but that was Tagora's affair. We had cut the total weight of equipment considerably.

The rest of that afternoon and evening we spent trying to improve the path out of the clearing to the mountainside. There was a chain of small streams and boggy patches which had to be bridged. At least we should put the first part of the journey behind us dry-shod.

Throughout our last night in Rilo the stars shone brightly in a clear sky. It was ironical that the only luck we had with the weather on the whole of our expedition was that which covered our dismal retreat.

CHAPTER XIX

# Rilo—Seidjhosa

THE NEXT MORNING WE WERE UP BEFORE DAWN. THE BURU
was forgotten for the time being; all our energies were
reserved for the difficulties of the journey home. Against
our expectations Tagora's team proved equal to their task.
There was the usual fuss as to who should carry what; but
old men and boys bent stoutly to the work, easing their heads
into their bark carrying bands and heaving each other to
their feet. It was a ragged line, but at least it was on the
move. A place was even found for Orenimo's wicker basket
full of cockerels. Orenimo had spent some time bartering
for these birds, and nothing would have persuaded him to
part from them, for each was possessed of a most strident
crow, an accomplishment unknown among the roosters of
his own Shillong homestead.

Our last act was to burn down all that remained of the
camp. Charles was adamant about this; nothing was to be
left for the Rilo Daflas. Only by teaching them this minor
lesson could we hope for better treatment for any party
which might follow us. At the height of the conflagration
Tapook arrived. A shadow of perplexity crossed his face as
he saw the fire, but if he was disappointed he did not show
it. He even seized a brand himself and helped us spread the
flames. My last sight of him as we moved across the clearing
at the end of the procession nearly brought a lump to my
throat. The camp was burning behind him. He had drawn
himself up to his full height and was slowly raising his right
arm in farewell. There were no words we could speak to
each other, but his face shone with an indescribably pathetic
expression. Had Tapook not had the misfortune to be born

the younger brother of a headman; had he been taken young and taught sympathetically, he could have become a real influence for good among the Daflas. But now he was set in his ways, too old to learn. The realisation of that fact showed in his eyes as he watched us, in whom his last chance was vested, abandon him.

The first stage of the journey went well. We even got through the tunnel covering the stream without a soaking. On the trek up we had reckoned that a European without a load, was barely the equal on the march of a Dafla carrying fifty pounds. Now, with many weeks of healthy activity behind us the Daflas were simply not in it. It was not long before we had passed the entire column and had taken the lead.

At the top of the first cliff we ran into the leeches. The sodden leaves which formed the floor of the path were alive with them. In patches they must have numbered at least six to a leaf. Another large variety, green in colour, waved at us waist-high from the bushes. Yet another kind, mercifully rare, were even larger still and were brilliantly striped. These occurred in small colonies. We had each prepared ourselves after his fashion. After my last experience in the swamp I had gone back to my old calf-high seaboots. Charles and Frank had soaked their socks in brine and stuffed their boots with tobacco leaves. Orenimo, Pio Pio and Washington carried pads of salt bound round the end of sticks. A touch of salt is enough to dislodge a leech and to burst it if it is already filled with blood. This is the best method to get them off one's clothes where, once on, they will stick as tenaciously as slimy rubber bands looped through the cloth. We hastened on, scarcely pausing to scrape them off our boots, for to stop for two or three was merely to invite attention by ten times the number. A leech bite makes a clean wound which can scarcely be felt. It is not toxic. The most unpleasant thing about it is that the leech injects some substance into the wound which causes it to bleed long after the leech itself is satiated and has dropped off the skin. Thus there comes a time when one's boots fill with blood and one squelches along in a dismal state of mind knowing that one can take no further action until the end of one's journey.

"Could leeches kill a person?" is a question which we debated along that wretched march. The answer must undoubtedly be "Yes", if one is unfortunate enough to suffer an accident which leaves one helpless and immobile in the jungle. Frank knew of a hunter, canoeing on Lake Pereira in Southern India, who had put in to a little frequented shore at midday for tiffin. It was a very substantial tiffin and after it he lay down to sleep under a tree. He woke up in hospital. Leeches had come upon him in his sleep, and he was already unconscious, and in danger of being bled to death by hundreds of them when he was luckily discovered.

Charles related that once, after having taken a short cut down an overgrown path in the Naga country during the rains, he himself, had collapsed from loss of blood after reaching his destination.

The normal, healthy traveller on a recognised path suffers little actual physical discomfort, but if he is a sensitive, imaginative person he can rack himself with mental tortures. All sorts of pictures come to one's mind—a patch of bare flesh covered by a dense mat of slimy, pulsating bodies, depending from urgent mouths! It is not good to dwell on such things.

The leeches served one good purpose; hour after hour we pressed on at a good pace, never stopping. After us plodded the porters, daos in hand, scraping the leeches from their shins with the blade and winkling them out from between their toes with the point.

Early in the afternoon we topped the final ridge and could already hear the low mutter of the Upper Pakke River, thousands of feet below us. It had again begun to rain. I

was in the lead at this point and coming hurriedly round a
rock I stepped right into the middle of a nest of baby snakes.
They slithered round my boots and off the path.into the
jungle. I felt the mother must be about, but did not stop to
look.

Down by the water we reached our first main obstacle.
The river forked to go round the central island on which
stood the camping-ground. The right fork was the narrower
by far, but there the water was running deep and swift over
the stepping-stones we had used on our journey up. Just
beyond the stones the stream fell into a very considerable
rapid. It was obvious that the crossing might cost us men
as well as stores. The alternative, which we negotiated
successfully after some debate, was to walk out into the main
bed of the stream and follow the course of the river down
to the flank of the island. The wider fork was far shallower,
but even then there were waist-deep pools, the current was
strong, and the bed was composed of loose, slippery
boulders. Recent flood wreckage along the banks showed
us a high-water mark that would have placed us utterly out
of our depth, and once more we blessed our changed luck
with the weather.

We stood cheerlessly in the rain among the ruins of our
first camp at Pakke waiting for the baggage to come up.
There were now leeches in plenty on the island, but our
main thought was to get into dry clothes. Luckily Washington was among the first to arrive, and with him he brought
the makings of a pot of tea. Without delay he performed the
miracle of lighting a fire out of the sodden material at hand.

Suddenly the mist lifted, the skies cleared and the sun
shone brilliantly once more. It beat upon us so fiercely that
our clothes rapidly dried on our backs, but with the bright-
ened light a cloud of dim-dams descended and stung us
unmercifully until we wished ourselves back in the jungle
gloom with the leeches. By this time we had exhausted all
our repellent oil, and the best protection we could think of

was an evil-smelling concoction of rancid butter and kerosene.

Also among the first arrivals was Orenimo with Kiro. The dog was as boisterous as ever, but he looked a sorry sight. His flanks were dappled with scarlet blood patches, while more leeches hung inside his nostrils and from his eye-lids. These took some time to deal with.

Throughout the late afternoon the Daflas straggled into camp in twos and threes. They had accomplished all that Tagora claimed they would, and it was uncanny to watch the surefootedness with which they waded the river under their heavy baskets. But we soon discovered that a large number of articles was missing from the loads. My moisture-proof tin with the last of my cigarettes was gone; so was the cord from Charles's pyjama trousers! Tagora whined piteously in disclaiming responsibility; Thai, his fellow headman looked genuinely distressed. There was no point in searching men who wore practically no clothes at all; in any case, it was obvious that anything which had disappeared from the loads would now be buried in some jungle cache waiting retrieval on the journey back to the hills. Pakke was no place to stage a showdown. The Daflas would be quite capable of deserting us where we were, in which case we should arrive in the plains with nothing of our equipment salvaged at all. We could only resign ourselves to further minor losses.

That evening while we bathed in the chill water, the Daflas constructed an excellent pole bridge over the main branch of the stream. Only a cloudburst overnight could prevent us from crossing the first main obstacle. A sudden prolonged storm such as many we had already experienced could still maroon us where we were until September, but all was well the next morning.

The bridge held until the last of the Daflas was over, then it collapsed under Charles, who, however, escaped with a ducking.

The trek up to Takko Senyak, which had seemed the easiest of all in the reverse direction by virtue of its being largely downhill, was the most exhausting of our return journey. Physically, the effort was well within our endurance, but in unchanging scenery it soon became unutterably monotonous; the long dragging ascents up interminable slopes; the sliding, jolting, twisting, descents which placed us ever again at the foot of a fresh climb. At times I almost felt like shouting at the sheer boredom of it.

We did not arrive in camp until mid-afternoon, and by that time drizzling rain had set in once more. Leeches had been far fewer along the march, but they were plentiful enough round the camp site, and we spent most of our time plucking them off our boots before they could reach our socks. It remains a complete mystery to us what leeches feed on when there is no flesh and blood at hand. They do not merely congregate on the jungle paths, they are spread just as evenly in their billions in the remoter recesses of the forest where no man or animal ever goes. And they do not feed on their own kind.

It was at Takko Senyak that our specimen insects met their terrible fate. We had cleared a wide area round the tents of fallen leaves, in order to keep the leeches at bay while we slept. In scraping the earth we must have disturbed a red ants' nest. Frank had set up a pole next to his tent, and on top of it had placed Tameng's specimen box. During the night the ants found the pole and swarming up it attacked the box. By morning the leaf-insect had lost its limbs, and was a tattered wreck of its former self. The same was the state of the stick insect and the praying mantis. All that was left of the splendid canary-coloured moth was a tiny heap of dust. There was nothing we could do about it, and we placed the box on the camp fire. It was the wretched manner in which the trapped creatures had met their death rather than their loss which oppressed us, and for the first time we sat down to a wordless breakfast. That day we walked down five thousand feet from the chill rain of the hills to the glaring heat of the plains. Leeches, dim-dams, sandflies, mithan flies were a thing of the past; all that we had now to endure were mosquitoes.

In the last mile a final tremendous thunderstorm overtook us. Each of us sought a tree and stood beneath its shelter waiting for the storm to pass, while a barking deer coughed spasmodically in the undergrowth near by. It was the last rain we experienced. Down at the Lenko site the sun shone brightly. Behind us the clouds hung in a thick dank shroud over the mountains through we which had come.

The stream through the ravine now offered a chain of idyllic bathing pools filled with foaming, ginger-beer coloured water. Frank and I spent the rest of that afternoon sprawled naked on the baking rocks occasionally rolling off them into the water when the sun grew too hot. Some fish were about in the pools and Frank collected the Mauser and tried to shoot a few. All that we achieved was to stun two or three which were too small for our cooking pot, but which the Daflas found no trouble in swallowing whole and alive. We went to bed that night healthily tired and blissfully clean.

The next day's march held three problems. Firstly, the heat, which was likely, easily to top one hundred degrees in the shade, a temperature to which the hill Daflas were entirely unaccustomed. Secondly, the lower reaches of the Pakke, which might already be unfordable. Thirdly, the making of our rendezvous with the truck transport. An early start was essential, and consequently we were on our way with the first light of dawn.

Beyond Lenko village we ran into trouble. The jungle swamp with its huge clumps of elephant grass and tall reeds had grown up beyond our expectations, reducing visibility to a few yards at the most. The ground underfoot was thick, oozing mud. There was no longer one trail, but many, all pointing in different directions. By this time the column was strung out in twos, threes and fours like the beads of a badly threaded necklace, and it was not long before groups in the centre and rear of the line began to get lost. Confusion was added to by the fact that both Tagora and Thai stopped off in the village to visit their old friend the Lenko priest. Charles stood impotently by the bank of the river with the head of the column waiting for stragglers to come in. The sun was mounting ever higher, precious minutes were being lost. The water was running deep and swiftly. It looked just fordable, but Charles decided not to take the risk. If we took the short cut over the stream, sooner or later we should have to recross it and no one knew what conditions were like farther down. Accordingly, when about half the party had collected, Charles led them off on a long detour down the near bank round the outside of the first bend. Frank and I doubled back into the swamp to whip in the remainder. It was already stiflingly hot in the swamp and the blades of the elephant grass slashed like swords at our hands and faces. After collecting half a dozen men we returned once more to the bank. Here we found that what we had tried to avoid had already happened. A large batch of men had passed us in the swamp, had reached the river and gone on across it. We were just in time to see Kiro land on the far shore about four hundred yards below the point where he had started from. There was nothing for it but to follow. It was not a difficult crossing. The water was barely waist-deep and holding hands to keep our balance we made short work of it. We made good time across the neck of the bend, and found the second ford even easier, for we crossed again at a point where a broad island lay in mid-stream.

So far, so good. We had gained a good half-hour over Charles's party, it seemed a pity not to make use of it. The porters with us were already panting and clamouring for a rest; I still felt reasonably fresh. It occurred to me that if one of us pressed on to Seidjhosa he could contact the truck drivers and all our troubles would be solved. If we all stayed where we were there was a good chance that the drivers would tire of waiting and turn for home. I decided to go on, but as I was not entirely sure of the way, for the aspect of the whole countryside had changed, I called for a volunteer. Thai at once stepped forward and we set off together.

The first mile or so down the bank of the river was straightforward enough. Then Thai began to falter and cast around. Sometimes he would double into the jungle, then come back to the stream, all the while intently peering at the ground. It soon dawned on me he was tracking and that he, himself, had no idea of the way. Worse still, he missed so many clearly defined footprints, it became additionally obvious that he must be near-blind. It seemed strange to me that I had not spotted this before but the answer is probably that the affliction is far less apparent in a primitive person than in a civilised one. We stood no chance of becoming utterly lost, but now we might well be last, and not first, at Seidjhosa. At this I patted Thai on the back and led the way. The footprints turned once more to the river's edge and continued across a line of sandbanks. Then they disappeared at the water's edge. This seemed to strike a familiar chord in Thai's mind, and the old man, in his now-bedraggled scarlet cloak, set off once more across the river. I followed very dubiously. I did not remember the crossing from the journey up, but I thought it just possible that Thai knew an alternative and better route. On the far bank once more, Thai set a cracking pace downstream. The footprints were clear for some distance, then we lost them over a patch of rock. Still Thai pressed on. I was now certain that we had come well past the point on the other bank where we should have turned off into the jungle. There was nothing for it but to get back over the river. Thai agreed, but now we had lost all the advantage of shallow fords. Opposite us the river cut hard into a steep cliff; it looked the worst possible place for a crossing but Thai plunged in without any further ado. Possibly he could not see what lay before him. I never saw how he got across for soon I was fully occupied with my own progress. The water pressed like a solid wall against my chest. At times I was so nearly off my balance that I was convinced that only the minute pressure of my big toe against a stone kept me upright. In normal strength I could have swum it fully clothed, but with my left arm still as weak as it was, I could have made no progress against that current, and should merely have floated endlessly downstream. Foot by foot I made it until the last ten yards, then I was swept off my feet and landed in a heap with Thai against a submerged tree trunk.

We had now lost all the time we had gained, and more, and it was with some chagrin that on looking upstream I saw Charles, in his white shirt, turn off into the jungle about a mile above us. By the time we had returned to that point by climbing painfully along the cliff face, Charles must have been a good forty minutes ahead. Thai now began to flag badly. It was approaching noon, and the oppressive heat on top of his exertions had drained the strength out of him. He sat down gasping by the waterside reluctant to move. Frank, I could see a quarter of a mile away chivvying along the porters. I did not wait but pushed on alone. I was soon sorry I had done so; it was no joke breaking the trail along the jungle avenue. The grass now grew chest-high and again the old fear of treading on a snake came over me. I would have given up had I not known that Charles was somewhere in front. After a short distance the grass thinned again, and I came on a better defined trail between the tall jungle curtains. This jungle of the plains was utterly unlike that of the hills. In the mountains one is overcome by a feeling of complete loneliness; here one sensed the teeming life and stealthy movement on either side behind the curtains, although there was no sound other than the clatter of a Great Hornbill in branches high above. I wished that clown of the forest well on its way before the Daflas came up, for it carried enough black and white barred feathers to stock a cap shop.

In patches the turf beneath my feet was scuffed with the shovel-shaped scars of wild elephant. Before long I came on the fat pug marks of a tiger keeping to the dead centre of the track. These marks were very fresh, and for an uneasy moment I felt that the line of march must be Charles—the tiger—then myself. A moist hundred yards showed Charles's hob-nailed boot prints covering the tiger's spoor, and I breathed again. However, I cannot say that I felt any too happy along that three and a half miles, alone and armed only with a walking-stick, and it was not merely the blazing sun which discomforted me. I should have felt far less happy, and I believe the intrepid Charles would have felt less happy, too, had we known then what we learnt later, that a man-eating leopard was aprowl in the district and that a similar animal, if not the same one, had clawed Taning the year before on the same stretch of track.

I reached the point where the fork turned off towards the Seidjhosa camp site. Charles was nowhere to be seen either at the junction or by the ruined Dafla huts. And there were no trucks. I chose a shady tree by the jungle path and sat down and waited for Frank. As soon as he came up we debated the next move. We soon picked up Charles's tracks heading on to Lokra; but there were no wheel marks to be seen. Either our message had not reached Menzies or the trucks were stuck farther down the road. The question was how far? We were not worried about Charles. Another five miles would bring him to the first tea-gardens and if necessary he could put up with a planter for the night. But by now it had become intolerably hot and we shirked the responsibility of flogging the porters on indefinitely beyond their normal day's stage. Night might well find us still in the jungle. That sort of jungle is reasonably safe during the day time for human beings, but as soon as dusk came it would be a very different matter.

The question was settled for us by the porters themselves. As soon as they reached us they dumped their loads and flatly refused to go farther. They were not used to the intense heat, they had been taxed beyond their normal endurance and there could be no blaming them. We decided to camp once more in the open down by the river and wait for Charles and the trucks to collect us.

The water soothed our immediate worries. Opposite the camp site a lagoon the colour of clouded jade spilled over from the main stream and flowed round beneath the trees which shaded us. The river was no longer our enemy. In no time Frank, I, Orenimo, Pio Pio, Washington, the two Gurkhas and all the Daflas were revelling in it. Six miles up stream it had still been chilly, but here under the full glare of the sun it was already luke-warm. It washed the caked sweat and mud of our bodies and put new strength into us.

Tea was a tricky affair for wasps were swarming near by and all of us were stung repeatedly, but that was a minor drawback. The afternoon roll call showed that three of the Daflas were missing. One was a stalwart young man, the pick of the bunch, who had been carrying my ruck-sack and Orenimo's cockerels; the remaining couple were an unsavoury pair, inseparable companions whom we had always suspected. The first was a squat, ungainly hunchback, the second a gaunt villainous-looking man whose dark skin denoted slave parentage. He limped under the handicap of a gaping shin ulcer. It so turned out that we deeply wronged this couple in thinking that they had deserted us. Tagora and Pio Pio who went out to look for them found them waiting over two miles down the Lokra road. They had gone on unquestioningly beyond the junction; a stout effort, which we duly rewarded when we retrieved them. The third was recovered the next day. He had pressed on untiringly and actually caught up with Charles.

That evening Thai warned us that a feud had broken among the Daflas and that there might be trouble. He was quite right. Dusk had hardly fallen when there was a sudden uproar round the porters' camp fire, and in a second, two men were fighting like wild cats on the ground, scattering embers in all directions. Thai, Frank and I jumped on them before fighting could become general and tore them apart. We never knew what started the fight; probably a dispute over possession of some of the belongings which had been looted from us. Wounds were fairly evenly divided. One man had a deep cut over the left eye; the other had a wrenched shoulder and two broken bones in his hand. We quashed further trouble by making an elaborate show of dressing the injuries. Frank dealt with the eye; I made a sling for the shoulder out of an old escape map of France, which was entirely meaningless to the wearer, but caused a good deal of curiosity and envy among his companions. The diversion was sufficient to still passions for the night, but Frank and I agreed that it would be better to get the men on the move early the next morning rather than risk another day in idleness.

# CHAPTER XX

# The Buru of the "Hindusthan Standard"

AT DAWN, WE HAD SCARCELY STARTED OUT, WHEN WE MET Charles striding towards us through the elephant grass. He reported that the trucks were held up by a broken bridge four miles down the road and were now waiting for us. My missing rucksack had arrived. But that was not his main news. In his hand he waved a letter from Menzies, and a newspaper cutting brought to him by one of the drivers. "Something dreadful has happened, dreadful," he exclaimed, while his face looked a picture of consternation. "Read this," he said, handing me the cutting.

It was from the *Hindusthan Standard* of 5th May and ran:

### "EXTINCT" MAMMAL'S STRIDE ALONG HIMALAYAN BORDER

#### "From our Shillong Office"

A Dinotherium, a member of a race of huge, prehistoric mammals, till now believed to be totally extinct, has been seen perambulating in the southern side of the Himalayan Range bordering on Assam, according to reports reaching here. Tribal people of the frontier tract of Balipara recently came across this moving mountain of flesh wandering majestically and happily plucking the tops of huge, ancient trees.

Though its exact shape, habits and other details are not at present available and contradictory reports vie with one another in exaggeration, there seems to be striking unanimity as to its stature which is said to be about 90 feet long and 20 feet high. Most of the evidence is negative. Its face resembles nothing that is known or can be imagined, while its posterior is like the tail of a lizard, or to be more precise, what it would be if magnified a billion billion times. It has no tusks—at least it does not show them—and its footprints are authoritatively learnt not to be those of an elephant. It is said to be very decent in its dealing as it did not damage or destroy the crops or kill a single mortal when it visited several outlying tribal areas. The people are, however, scared and are evacuating some of the villages. The Political Officer in the Balipara frontier tract has, it is understood, been directed by the Assam Government to keep constant watch over the movement of this curious stranger, and several observers have already been employed to collect more precise details. Adequate precautionary measures have been taken to see that the tribals do not destroy this animal or tease it away into some inaccessible region of the Himalayan Range, making further authoritative scrutiny impossible.

Services of expert zoologists are being requisitioned and a preliminary account has already been, it is gathered, sent to the Royal Zoological Society in London. An official account from the Assam Government is not expected immediately till full investigations are completed, and they are satisfied that really an unusual specimen of life is abroad.

The note from Menzies was terse and to the point: "I'm being snowed under with inquiries; for God's sake come and get me out of it!"

It was easy to understand Charles's indignation. Left to ourselves we could still have published our account of the buru, for what it was worth, on a basis of scientific fact. But now someone in Shillong, who knew only half the story, had talked and it looked as if Charles's two years of patient, conscientious investigation was to end in ludicrous fiasco. For us the buru might be as dead as the dodo; but for the world, in absurd, grotesque form it had only just begun to live!

Frank and I laughed heartily in spite of ourselves. I had been well and truly "scooped" on my own story. But as one professional journalist, examining the work of another, I could only bow in deference to my conqueror. He had been unscrupulous, it is true, but nevertheless, he had done a magnificent job of work. "Leaving out the biological aspect", as Charles would have said, there was enough of solid truth in the story to make a first-class sensation.

No one in Shillong could deny that there was good reason to believe that "an unusual specimen of life is abroad"— that the services of an expert zoologist had been requisitioned to trace it—that a preliminary account had already been sent to London. Having established those indisputable facts the author was free to draw on his imagination, and what a good job he had made of it! He had scored his point. He had merely to wait until our investigations were completed, and then he could not lose either way.

As we hurried along that last four miles through the jungle Frank and I tried to console ourselves with working out that given a lizard's tail as of length three inches, the buru's posterior, a billion billion times the size, would stretch from Assam to the moon and beyond! We were so engrossed in this calculation that, unwittingly, we walked through a patch of the large striped leeches clinging to the dewy grass. We had packed our boots and were walking in gym shoes, and we did not notice the leeches until they were stuck fast to our trouser ends and bare ankles.

We reached the trucks in good order, paid off Tagora's team and left them squabbling over the remainder of the rice. We were over the Bharelly ferry by midday and paused only in the lines of the Assam Rifles to look up Frank Noble. Frank was out, but we raided his canteen to the tune of a case of beer and a bottle of gin. Menzies was in, and a glance at his file showed us his dilemma. Letters containing inquiries, advice, and offers of help in tracking down the monster were pouring in from all over India and from overseas. There was even a cable from Buenos Aires. A foreign correspondent of high repute in New Delhi wrote that he had received an irate message from London asking: "Why the devil aren't you in Assam." The representative of a news agency in Calcutta, beaten by the initial story, had introduced a sex angle by "discovering" the monster's mate! Still another enterprising journalist had linked the "monster" with the Abominable Snowman. Planters in the Balipara area had posted guards round their tea-gardens; there were rumours that Noble's Assam Rifles had been mobilised. Menzies, who only knew half the story himself owing to his absence when we had first arrived at Lokra, had been summoned to Shillong. There was still a faint hope in Government circles that a "monster" might appear, and thus the poor buru became the subject of an official communique stating that while it could not be confirmed that any such monster as described existed, investigations were being made and the results awaited. It was thought that by introducing an element of doubt, the more responsible news editors would shy away from the story; but it was by no means the end of the matter.

As for ourselves, we retired to the guest house, a three-roomed, thatched bungalow, open on all sides, and drowned our sorrows with the aid of the case of beer. I was in a particularly intricate predicament. It was an odds-on chance that my own story would be denied before I had a chance to write a line, in which case the interest would be dissipated, and I might just as well not bother about it. There was also a possibility that a boastful youth like Taning, if he found a ready audience, would invent a superb monster of his own, in which case I should be "scooped" again! I therefore sat down and wrote out a 2,000 word cable forthwith giving the whole history of the expedition. I walked with this the three miles to the Lokra Telegraph Office. The clerk there was about to shut down for the day; he had never seen a Press cable before; he was appalled at its length and I was hardly surprised when I learned later that not a word of it was ever received in London!

That evening Frank Noble arrived to drive us to the Planters' Club at Thakabari. It was soon apparent that we had underestimated the publicity given the buru. We had left in secret, but now everyone knew about us; we returned prominent figures, if not as yet popular heroes.

Conan Doyle's *Lost World* ends with the complete confusion of the critics, when to silence doubters, Professor Challenger releases a live pterodactyl during a mass meeting at the Queens' Hall, London. The good fellows of the Thakabari Club would not rest content with anything less spectacular. We were no longer expected to prove that the "monster" existed; we were led to the bar, and called upon to show good reason why it *did not* exist! Throughout that evening the ice chinked merrily for us in innumerable tall whisky and sodas. In the face of that overwhelming hospitality it was difficult, indeed, to preserve any correct sense of proportion. I could not relate the whole story; at least until my paper in London had had a fair chance to use it if they so wished. And then, although the idea of a 90-foot long animal was absurd, none of us was prepared to deny flatly that a buru of the more conservative proportions described by the Daflas might not still exist. On the map there was always that tempting patch of white between Rilo and the Apa Tanis. And if anybody could be found with the time, patience and money to excavate the burial sites in the Apa Tani valley there was always the prospect of a rich scientific reward.

It was regrettable that we had to leave that excellent club in the same state of suspense as we had found when we entered it. Long after my return to London I received a letter from Menzies which contained the following paragraph:

> It seems that more interest is being taken now in the "buru" after your departure than before. The public feel that the animal really does exist, and that our efforts in denying its existence is just a blind to keep away the inquisitive ones. Evidently they have swallowed the papers' version hook, line and sinker!

I hope that if ever a copy of this book reaches Thakabari we may be forgiven.

We clambered into bed that night with spinning heads; but the night was not yet over for Noble. Driving back to his quarters he came across a huge Banded Krait stretched across the road outside his go-down. He ran his car three times over it backwards and forwards before he could kill it, and he then left the body lying by the roadside. This incident had an odd sequel.

The next morning Frank drove down early to the lines of the Assam Rifles to shoot some film with Noble's help. Coming back to our bungalow to breakfast he picked up the dead Krait in order that we could measure it and take some pictures of it in our compound. It was a magnificent specimen with broad yellow and black stripes and measured fifty-two and a quarter inches. It was triangular in section, and would have been absolutely lethal if it had had a chance to bite anybody.

That day passed quietly enough. In the evening Frank and I drove out to dinner at a planter's bungalow, Charles remained behind to write letters.

The next morning he related that while he was sitting writing on the veranda he had heard a sudden commotion in the room occupied by Frank and himself, and had found that Kiro had got a second Banded Krait at bay between the two beds. He called out Orenimo and Pio Pio, and after a short chase they had killed the snake in the bathroom. This encounter at once caused us to revive the old tale that snakes always hunt in pairs. If this was evidence in support of that fact it was quite remarkable, for the two snakes had been killed at least four miles apart, and the arm of vengeance must be a deal sight longer than we had thought it was. Charles upset this theory with a far more unpleasant alternative; namely, if it was true that snakes hunted in pairs, what had probably happened was that we had killed one each of two pairs, in which case both Frank Noble and ourselves could expect another visitor!

# CHAPTER XXI

# We Leave Lokra

IT WAS OUR LAST MORNING AT LOKRA. FRANK AND I HAD arranged to leave on the early afternoon train. Owing to the leakage of information from Shillong I could no longer wait in a remote outpost; I must push on to Calcutta where I should be more easily accessible. News of the impending mithan sacrifice had come in, but this I had to leave to Charles. Orenimo, as permanent bearer, was to stay with Charles and travel with him to Shillong by jeep. Pio Pio and Washington were to accompany us as far as Rangiya; there they were to change trains for Shillong. Taning and Tameng came in to say "Good-bye" and to receive their bakshish. Tameng was grinning all over his face; he was dressed in new drill trousers and his long black locks fell over a clean white shirt. I had no qualms about Tameng. For him the jungle, only a few hundred yards away, represented a vast store-house of raw materials. From it he could weave all manner of baskets and carrying bags; could cut cane, twist rope. There was unlimited bamboo waiting to be fashioned into a wide variety of utensils. He could gather scores of different kinds of edible plants and fungi. He could collect feathers and skins. He had a ready market in the Lokra sepoys and the indolent Dafla settlers. If ever his market failed, all he need do would be to drift back into the jungle where he would have only himself to provide for. The jungle was his life and his natural home.

Neither had I any fears for Taning. He had all the push and the self-confidence in the world. When he was a little more mature he would make a first-class interpreter; youths of his quick wit and intelligence were rare enough among the Daflas. They were in great demand.

We bade farewell to Charles on the platform at Rangipara (North). Once more Frank and I were back in a rocking, narrow gauge, railway carriage. After the clean, cool air of the mountains we felt grievously hot, sticky and dirty. For a long time, in the distance, we saw the blue ranges of the Balipara hills and the notch in them cut by the Pakke River, where the trail led up to Rilo.

Close to the railway track the green panorama of the jungle rolled past us for the last time. As we chugged along I recognised this familiar situation and that; for the jungle has little variety when one is accustomed to it. It no longer held nameless terrors for me. I had almost overcome my old fear of snakes; I had mastered my new-found loathing of leeches. There were many other things I did not like about it; but nevertheless I was now in sympathy with it. I felt that if an airplane force-landed me in any patch of jungle anywhere, provided I was still sound of limb, I should have a reasonable chance of walking out of it alive. That, I felt, was knowledge worth acquiring, even if I was never to need it again.

We reached Rangiya in the evening light. It was the same shrill bustling station scene one sees anywhere in India. Betel-nut-, food-, cigarette-, newspaper-sellers jostled with water-carriers to get at the train. They trod uncaringly on the same groups of inert, sleeping, cotton-swathed figures that lie around every Indian station apparently indifferent as to which train goes when, where, or why. Batches of small boys pressed close to the compartment piping five-year-old song-hits or brandishing boxes of boot brushes and lisping "Su Sin, Sa'b", (Shoe-shine, Sahib?)—routines they had first learnt when British and American troops were passing to and from the Burma Front. In a far corner a dusty bear weaved restively at the end of the heavy metal chain by which it had been dragged out of the mountains.

The time came to say "Good-bye" to Pio Pio and Washington. Both had been engaged as casual workers; for a brief space they had known security, food in plenty, and good companionship. Now, neither knew when he would find work again. There was nothing sheepish in the manner in which they approached us, they knew that for a few minutes more they were still among friends, but in their eyes I caught the same fleeting agonised expression which I had last seen in the eyes of Tapook; the realisation that a good era was passing, and that dreadful insecurity was again at hand. I pressed on them all the money I could spare, and shook each warmly by the hand as man to man. Then the train jolted forward once more, and they were left to their own devices in the violet dusk.


THE END